LANGUAGE AND RULES

JANUA LINGUARUM

STUDIA MEMORIAE
NICOLAI VAN WIJK DEDICATA

edenda curat

C. H. VAN SCHOONEVELD

INDIANA UNIVERSITY

SERIES MINOR

80

1970

MOUTON

THE HAGUE · PARIS

LANGUAGE
AND
RULES

by

JON WHEATLEY

UNIVERSITY OF CALIFORNIA

1970

MOUTON

THE HAGUE · PARIS

LIBRARY OF CONGRESS CATALOG CARD NUMBER: 70-95011

Printed in The Netherlands by Mouton & Co., Printers, The Hague

ACKNOWLEDGEMENTS

I would like to acknowledge the support I received from Queen's University in doing the computer work involved in this project: in particular, for awarding me a Summer Research Associateship during 1964; for money I received from the Arts Research Committee for the purchase of materials; and for free use of computer time at the Computing Centre.

Parts of Chapter 7 and Appendix III appeared in *Dialogue* and *Theoria*. I would like to thank the editors of these journals for permission to reprint the material here.

I would also like to acknowledge the help, encouragement and succor I received from Miss Valerie Howell during the writing of the computer program. Without her help, the project would never have been completed. Finally, I would like to thank Mr. Fred Heap who first got me seriously interested in computers and taught me how to program them.

JON WHEATLEY

FOREWORD

This monograph is intended equally for philosophers and linguists. This involves no compromises, except that technical terms peculiar to either discipline are defined. The ground covered here represents a join between linguistics and the philosophy of language without being outside, or even on the borderlines of, either. The monograph is obviously directed to linguists. It is worth saying, therefore, that the only thing atypical about it as a work in the philosophy of language is this: that some of the theories about language offered are substantiated in more ways than just by argument; in particular, a pilot computer program has been written to analyse language on the basis of these theories and the theories receive support from the fact that the program runs successfully (it is described in the final chapter). This does not imply that the theories are unphilosophical, only that they are precise.

TABLE OF CONTENTS

1

INTRODUCTION

Using language and learning language are rule guided activities. If we could state the rules used in learning and using any language we would have given the grammar of that language; we would have given much else besides.

There are two difficulties about stating the rules involved in language learning and language using. First, analysing the language one already speaks is psychologically very difficult. One formulates a rule or a definition and claims that it fits one's practice. What one often does not notice is that the rule or the definition is so vague, or so lacking in explanatory power, that it would fit virtually any practice. Consider the definition A SENTENCE IS A COMPLETE THOUGHT. Once one thinks about it, it is surely obvious that a COMPLETE THOUGHT, considered independently of sentences, is just not the sort of thing which is identifiable. What is the case is that we can all identify sentences and non-sentences perfectly well.[1] Furthermore, once this identification has taken place, it seems reasonable to characterise the sentences so identified as expressing complete thoughts. But the definition is totally lacking in explanatory power; there is no question of our being able to identify sentences by first identifying complete thoughts.

The second difficulty is this: that, being human, we tend to carry out the analyses which become our basis for generalization on too small a segment of the language we are considering.

The obvious way to avoid the first difficulty is to find some way

[1] Some linguists want to deny this position. I discuss the matter fully in Chapter 6.

to apply rules and definitions entirely mechanically. This guarantees both that they genuinely say something and that the claim that our practice does conform to them is valid. Technology is already ahead of this chain of reasoning: the modern digital computer is an ideal rule-following mechanism. It also works very quickly, which opens the way to the solution of the second difficulty. These are the considerations which made me interested in writing a language learning and analysis program for the computer.

In such a project, theory and practice get inextricably intertwined. From the theoretical considerations given above, one moves to the practical problem of formulating rules and definitions which are of a type which can be written into a computer program. This practical matter raises theoretical problems about the ways in which language could and should be analysed. If one finds what one hopes is a solution to these theoretical problems one faces the practical problem of actually writing the program for the computer. If the program can be written and does what it is supposed to do, then theory is at least partially confirmed.

This monograph contains the theoretical work necessary to the writing of a language learning and analysis program for the computer. At the end, I give an account of a pilot program which, granting that it is just a pilot program, does what it is supposed to do. Thus the monograph is primarily a theoretical work in linguistics and the philosophy of language, but also contains some practical grounds for supposing the theoretical part correct.

For reasons which will become apparent, the practical problem I set myself was as follows: to write a learning program for the computer which would take grammatically well formed sentences of the English language as data[2] and produce as output a 'dictionary' which would (a) list the words fed in as parts of the data sentences classified as to grammatical type and (b) go part of the way towards defining at least some of them in philosophically interesting ways. Although this was designed to be a learning program (i.e., a program where the computer ended up having information it was never

---

[2] In fact, a sub-set of grammatically well formed sentences. This is discussed in its place.

given) no attempt was made to simulate human learning; to do so is a completely different problem. Under fairly rigorous restrictions, the problem I set myself is solved. I have little doubt that the restrictions can be lifted with a larger computer than I had available and a much longer, though not theoretically more complex, program.

The work is laid out as follows: In the first two chapters, certain very general theories about language are discussed: several of these theories are incorrect and one is, I hope, correct. The point about the correct theory is that it contains very little. It is offered specifically as a theory containing all we need to say about language in general to get down to the data effectively. The next several chapters are devoted to a discussion of various semantic and syntactic problems. In such a discussion, it is conventional to discuss syntactics first and semantics second. I reverse the procedure for the following reason. It is my claim that linguists working on syntactics have made practical semantic mistakes which have injured their work. In order to point out these errors, and correct them, some semantic theory was needed. It was therefore developed first. In the chapters on syntactics, the principal concern is with various theories about the classification of words and the analysis of utterances, chiefly those theories associated with Noam Chomsky and C. C. Fries. I discuss these theories critically, not with the aim of either rejecting or accepting them wholly but with the idea of using them where they are sound and supplementing them where this is desirable and possible. I am then in a position to propound those items of theory which are needed to write the computer program. There follows an account of the program and the results of a test run; in the account of the program, information is provided on how it can be extended.

In language theory we write about language in language. A mistaken notion about how technical terms can be defined, and which terms require definition, can seriously hamper the theoretical work on linguistics which is being attempted. This was a difficulty which, I have claimed elsewhere,[3] Fries got himself into when he

---

[3] "Meaning and Meaningfulness in Fries", *Canadian Journal of Linguistics*, 1964. See also my "How to Give a Word a Meaning", *Theoria*, 1964.

was concerned with the notion of a sentence (it is discussed here in Chapter 6). In this monograph I have, therefore, been extremely careful about the key terms used. In most cases, I attempt to make use of ordinary words rather than esoteric or technical words: where I use a technical term, such as OPEN SENTENCE, I define it with some care. With other terms, such as VERBAL DEFINITION which is a very complex term to define, I indicate how a definition could be formulated. Care of this nature can be carried too far, though I hope I have not done so; it is certain, I think, that it has frequently not been carried far enough.

Throughout the monograph I try to give a minimum of theory rather than a maximum; the more economical our linguistic theories are the better they tend to be. I endeavour to work very close to the facts of language and to say what I have to say in the simplest possible way. The writing throughout is informal: work does not become more profound because its style is modeled on that of XIXth century German scholars. I have done everything in my power to keep it short; though knowledge is growing very fast today it is not growing at anything like the rate at which the volume of printed material is growing. The chapters have been kept very short so that there is a real unity to all the material in any one chapter. This, in turn, allows me to give the chapters titles which are genuinely informative as to the content of the chapter. The work is, in the most literal sense, a monograph. I deliberately do not follow up side-paths, however interesting they may look. To take the most obvious examples, I discuss only those aspects of semantic theory and language rules that are directly applicable to my final aim.

One organizational note: italics are used exclusively for sample words or sentences in the body of the text. Minimum references are frequently given in the body of the text; full bibliographical information is supplied in the Bibliography.

2

SOME THEORIES ABOUT LANGUAGE

Work on language has, in the past, been frequently vitiated because certain theories have been held to be so obvious as to need neither justification nor discussion. Sometimes, indeed, such theories are regarded as so obvious that they are not even stated, though they form the suppressed major premiss in central arguments. It is important for the work presented in this monograph that no such theories are presupposed. I therefore list a few of the more common of these theories below and give, in outline only, the reasons why the theories are wrong. One might add that it is well known that these theories are wrong, but not widely known: they seem to crop up again and again. When there is a detailed refutation of one of these theories in the literature I give a reference to it in brackets.[1]

The theories:

(1) WORDS ARE NAMES: If names are names, then common nouns, adjectives, etc. are not names. If someone says *The President of the United States is Mr. Johnson*, he has given the president's name; if he says *The President of the United States is a man* he has given the president's sex not his name: the word *man* is not a name. In other respects also this theory is just perverse. The crucial difference between names and common nouns is this: that a common noun can be correctly applied to many different things where a name can

---

[1] The theories considered here are all obviously wrong, once one looks at them carefully, and it is therefore easy to give an outline refutation. However there are several more sophisticated theories out today, one of these at least contrary to the semantic theses of this monograph. I discuss the most important of these in Appendix III.

be correctly applied to only one thing. Yet it is just this crucial difference that the theory that nouns are names, or the theory that words are names, ignores (See Ryle, "The Theory of Meaning"). If, then, words are not names the way proper nouns are names, in what way are they names? The standard answer is to say that they are names because they stand for things. That theory we will now consider.

(2) WORDS STAND FOR THINGS. If a word stands for something, and is thereby meaningful, we can quite reasonably ask what thing it stands for. Take the word *table*. What thing does it stand for? Clearly not this table I am now writing at, for if this table were destroyed the word *table* would not have its meaning destroyed. Nor can it stand for all the tables there are for that is not a thing but a collection of things. Equally, if it did stand for all the tables there are the word would change meaning every time a new table were built or an old one destroyed. Again, if the word *table* stood for every table, how could we ever talk about a particular table; we would have no way of referring to it. (See Wittgenstein, *Philosophical Investigations*; Ryle, "The Theory of Meaning"). Faced with these criticisms, proponents of the theory that words stand for things generally change the sort of thing for which they say words stand. They now adopt the theory that words are meaningful because they stand for ideas in someone's mind. That theory we will now consider.

(3) WORDS STAND FOR IDEAS. Again, one wants to ask, whose ideas? Yours and mine? So we mean different things by every word we use; that is, when two different people use the word *table*, *table* in its two uses stands for different ideas. Furthermore, ideas in the mind are private; one person's ideas are not necessarily like those of another person. So if words mean something because they stand for ideas, then every word is as many times ambiguous as there are speakers of the language. Nor is it a way out to say our ideas are at least similar because we describe them in the same way. When we describe something we do so in words, and words (we are told)

stand for ideas in our minds. Therefore, using the same words in the description as another uses is no guarantee that the ideas are even similar (See Alston, *Philosophy of Language*).

The notion which causes much of the difficulty in these last two theories is the notion of STANDS FOR. Pronouns stand for nouns, it is sometimes said. What is meant by this, I think, is that a certain noun (or noun phrase) can replace the pronoun in any given utterance without altering what is said. This is true of some pronouns (it is not, of course, true for all: *my* is a pronoun and no noun simpliciter can replace it, only a noun in the genitive case; and a noun in the genitive case has the functional properties of an adjective). In the sense of STANDS FOR where at least some pronouns stand for nouns or noun phrases, the phrase makes perfectly good sense. But in this sense of STANDS FOR it is obviously false that words stand for things or ideas; it is not just that they do not, it is logically impossible that they should. There does not seem to be any other suitable meaning for STANDS FOR which makes any sense out of the theories that words are meaningful because they stand for things or ideas (See Wittgenstein, *Philosophical Investigations*; Ryle, *The Concept of Mind*).

(4) WORDS ARE SIGNS. As with the previous two theories, we must ask what words could be signs of (for)? The theory has more plausibility than the last two because words can perfectly well be used as signs, and indeed often are. That is, PIZZA outside a place of business is a sign; *35* over a boarding area in an airport is a sign. But these are words used as signs (*pizza* is not always a sign), not words used as they are always used. Equally some words or phrases signify things, or anyway refer to things: for instance proper nouns and most phrases of the type *The first dog to be born at sea* refer to things. But though these words and phrases do refer to things they are not signs for these things, which is an entirely different matter. This theory is a slightly more plausible variant on the theory that every word is a proper noun and is incorrect for the same reasons that that theory is incorrect.

(5) AN UTTERANCE IS AN ENCODED MESSAGE.[2] This theory is a modern manifestation of an old and ubiquitous philosophical theory: that a human being doing anything other than on the basis of stimulus-response (i.e., doing it consciously) is doing two things: thinking and acting. Thus driving a car carefully consists of driving the car and taking care; acting intentionally consists in thinking out what one is going to do and then doing it. On this theory, speaking, which is an intelligent and conscious activity after all, consists in making up a message and then encoding it. The errors in this theory run so deep that it is impossible to go into them here. I shall therefore make just two points. (a) Although we sometimes do have intentions and later act them out it is quite clear that we often act intentionally without going through any such process. When I enter my room and turn on the light, I do not think about turning on the light before doing so, yet there is no sense in which I do not turn the light on intentionally. (b) The notion of ENCODE hangs loose when we talk of encoding a thought into language. One can encode a piece of English into Morse code, of course; there is a correspondence between elements of the language and bits of the code. But what does encoding a thought amount to? Presumably annexing to each thought or idea the corresponding word. So here the theory entails a variant of the theory that words stand for ideas (see Ryle, *Concept of Mind*).

(6) THE PRIMARY (SOLE) FUNCTION OF LANGUAGE IS TO X. There is no value for X such that the theory is both informative and correct. There is a sense in which one can substitute COMMUNICATE for X, but this is uninformative. All other substitutions which have been offered (STATE FACTS, INFORM, COMMUNICATE OUR EMOTIONS, COMMUNICATE OUR IDEAS, etc.) are incorrect and for the same reason: language has no prime or sole function; it is a human institution whose 'function' is to do what anyone can successfully make it do.

---

[2]   This theory is so far from dead that it is accepted, as so obvious as to need no discussion whatever, by Katz in *The Philosophy of Language*. What is so depressing is not that a theory well known to be wrong should be used but that it should be accepted with no discussion whatever.

The trouble with these theories is not so much that they are incorrect but that they are ambiguous. A proponent of one of them tends, in defending the theory, to broaden the meaning of one or more of the key terms (SIGN, STAND FOR, IDEA, MESSAGE, ENCODE) until the theory becomes vacuous; when he says *Words are signs* he does not mean that words have the properties of signs at all, or so it seems in discussion; what he means, he would have us believe, is that he proposes to use SIGN synonymously with WORD. But then, when the theory is no longer being defended, the meanings of the terms contract again and we get, for instance, talk of SIGN AND THING-SIGNIFIED, which is incorrect and grossly misleading.

3

THE NATURE OF LANGUAGE

In this chapter two descriptions of language will be given. The first is highly general and therefore not particularly informative. The second, which is less general, is more informative. As a consequence, it is the second with which we will work throughout the monograph. Being less general, the second description does not cover any conceivable language whatever. However, it does cover most indo-european languages, which is sufficient for the present purposes.

DESCRIPTION OF LANGUAGE I: A language, as a minimum, consists in (a) a finite morphemic vocabulary, (b) a finite set of rules for the combination of morphemes into possible utterances.

It is worth emphasizing that the vocabulary of any language must be finite or it would be unlearnable (which is to say, not a language). For the same reason, the number of rules must be finite. However, there is no necessity for the number of sentences to be finite. So long as there is no limit to the number of times a rule can be applied (i.e., so long as the rules are recursive) it is perfectly possible to generate an infinite set of sentences from a finite vocabulary using a finite number of rules. The system of ordinary whole numbers is of this nature. Starting with a vocabulary of about fifty words (which is far larger than is theoretically necessary) and with formation rules giving, in general, the way to form the number next higher than any given number, we can theoretically generate the infinite set of whole numbers.[1] Rules for possible utterance generation will,

[1] This has nothing to do with Peano's axioms. I am here concerned with how

of course, be a good deal more complex than this, but the principal is identical.

The description of language given above is not a definition. That is, though it does give two necessary conditions for language it does not give sufficient conditions. The most obvious sufficient condition lacking is this: that in order to have a language we must have something to talk about; a formal system is not a language. There are also other sufficient conditions lacking.

The notion of MORPHEME as used in the description given is not well defined; nor is it well defined in linguistic theory. As usually conceived, a morpheme is said to be the smallest unit of meaning. Thus *table*, *dog*, *a* are morphemes, as are *-s*, *-ed*. But of course *-s* and *-ed* are not morphemes every time they appear, e.g., *-s* is not a morpheme in *thesis*, nor *-ed* in *bed*. I suspect that, for language theory in general, the notion of a morpheme can never be well defined; that is, we will never be able to say anything more precise than that it is the smallest unit of meaning, which, depending as it does on the notion of MEANING, is highly obscure.[2] This is not important so long as it is recognized; the price we pay for generality is lack of specificity. However, for more practical work we need more precise terminology. Working with the majority of indo-european languages such a terminology is readily available: we have a vocabulary of WORDS. In fact we have what amounts to two vocabularies: an extended vocabulary which contains every word which can possibly be used significantly in an utterance (i.e., contains *cats* as well as *cat*, *greatest* as well as *great*); and a contracted vocabulary which has the property that the extended vocabulary

---

we might generate the set of whole numbers considered as items of English and with no particular reference to theories of the foundations of mathematics. Not every language has this potential so it serves as no more than an example.

[2] The crucial thing about a morpheme is that it is movable: that is, it can appear in certain types of rules for morphological variation. If the notion were to be well defined this would be the way to do it. However, it would be a redefinition, for semantically uncompounded words would not be morphemes under this definition: words appear in a different position in rules for morphological variation than do morphemes (as redefined). The changes brought about by this redefinition would be beneficial.

can be generated from it by a set of rules. In general, I shall use the term VOCABULARY in the sense of the contracted vocabulary. We must notice the elementary point that to use a language effectively it is necessary to command not only the vocabulary but also the rules (call them RULES FOR MORPHOLOGICAL VARIATION) by which the extended vocabulary can be generated.

With this point in mind, we can now produce a more specific description of language applicable at least to most indo-european languages.

DESCRIPTION OF LANGUAGE II: (applicable to most indo-european languages): A language, as a minimum, consists in (a) a finite vocabulary, (b) a finite set of rules for the formation of morphological variations on the words in this vocabulary, (c) rules for the combination of these words and their morphological variants into possible utterances. The (b) and (c) conditions combine more than is at first apparent. A rule of type (c) may well require the application of a rule of type (b).

The difference between the two descriptions given amounts to this: There is no necessity for a language to have a finite vocabulary so long as the set of morphemes it contains (granting the obscurity of the notion of a morpheme defined over all languages) is finite. There is, in fact, no necessity for the concept of a word at all, i.e., utterances of the language could consist in combinations of morphemes with no isolable words. Thus the (a) condition of Description II is insufficiently general. Equally, there is no necessity for a notion of morphological variation so the (b) condition of Description II is not entirely general. However, Description II is clearly a special case of Description I and, being more specific, is a great deal easier to work with. For this reason, I use it in what follows. Description II, in the same way as Description I, does not, of course, give sufficient conditions for the notion of a language.

There are two major difficulties associated with the second description given above. First, the notion of a vocabulary item, i.e., a meaningful word, is still obscure. One can say that a word is meaningful because there are rules for its correct employment.

However this merely puts the weight on the second difficulty which is that the nature of language rules is still totally obscure. These are major problems. It will be my task in the next several chapters to unpack the notion of a language rule, encompassing within that phrase both syntactic or grammatical rules, and semantic or logical rules. I shall first consider the notion of a language rule in general.

4

SOME PROPERTIES OF LANGUAGE RULES

Language using is a rule guided activity. However, the nature of a rule and the notion of breaking a rule[1] are not well understood. I shall first give some general properties of rules and then discuss two different types of rule. In the next chapter, I shall offer a discussion of certain types of semantic rule.

A rule is not an order and it need not be expressed in the linguistic form of an imperative. Most often a rule has the linguistic form of a simple statement of fact. For instance,

> *The king (in chess) moves one square in any direction unless blocked by another piece of the same colour.*

Most language rules are most easily expressed in this way.

Not all rules can be broken. For instance, rules giving the procedure to be followed in gaining some end cannot, in some cases but not in all, be broken. The rule,

> *Students may petition to drop a course before mid-semester without suffering a grade penalty,*

cannot be broken, though someone may fail to invoke such a rule when it would be to his advantage to do so. The language rule discussed in the next paragraph is of this type.

---

[1] Philosophers have traditionally focused on the notion of FOLLOWING A RULE. But as Wittgenstein pointed out in connection with such basic human activities as language use, following a rule is just to act (normally, understandably, appropriately). What is of more interest in this context is the notion of breaking a rule.

Within language there appears to be an over-riding procedural rule of this type,

> *If some rule (which can be broken) is* obviously *broken, look for the explanation and act sensibly in the light of it.*

This is perhaps an over-riding rule on all rule governed or guided activities.[2] Thus when a Rugby scholar first picked up the ball and ran with it, he broke a rule of soccer and thereby invented rugger. However, it is in the area of language using that this rule is most often invoked. We self-consciously bestow praise and prizes on those who break language rules in interesting sorts of ways. That is, some poets, philosophers and religious teachers break language rules in ways which are considered to be most important and interesting. However, it is not only in the writings of poets that this rule is invoked. The first person who used the phrase *bachelor girl* was doubtless understood, and so was the person who first spoke of something being *very excellent*, though both were breaking semantic rules. Equally, someone who says of some meat dish *It tastes like potted donkey* (though he has no idea what donkey tastes like)[3] is not misunderstood. OBVIOUSLY breaking a language rule is often perfectly understandable and expressiveness is sometimes gained by so doing. I shall call this rule the OVER-RIDING RULE. This rule is used more often than one realizes at first glance (for instance, in a great many evaluative utterances) and is one of the chief agents in the evolution of language.

It is worth noticing that the Over-riding Rule is more often invoked than it is understood. If the Over-riding Rule is to be successfully invoked, then looking for the explanation for breaking the rule must be an activity which is, at least for most people, one which is crowned with success. This is the case with most uses of *bachelor girl* but it is dubiously the case with "The Absolute enters into, but is itself incapable of, evolution and progress" (Bradley, *Appearance*

---

[2] Notice how the practice of civil disobedience invokes, or attempts to invoke, this rule.

[3] The rule broken here is of the type discussed towards the end of this chapter and in more detail at the end of the next chapter. It is given explicitly at the end of the next chapter (#1).

and Reality). Philosophers have been some of the worst offenders in misusing the Over-riding Rule.

It is important to recognize the existence of the Over-riding Rule because it is important to notice other distinctions between rules, and what happens when they are broken, which have nothing to do with the Over-riding Rule. Below I develop a distinction between two different types of rule which depends on the sorts of things which happen when they are broken.

There are, within language, rules like the rules of chess. These rules, if broken and if the Over-riding Rule is not being invoked, tend to vitiate the enterprise on which one is engaged. If a player in chess moves his Rook in the way designated for moving a Bishop then, if he does not take the move back, the game is at an end; the game of chess does not include provisions for the circumstance that a rule is broken except to say, by implication, that the game now being played is not chess. I call these INDEFEASIBLE RULES. For some reason, all language rules have often been construed on the model of indefeasible rules. It is true that many grammatical rules should be construed on this model but not true that all logical (semantic) rules should be.

Most rough-and-tumble games, as well as having indefeasible rules, also have rules which are regularly broken without vitiating anything. It is on these occasions that the referee blows his whistle and calls for a new first down, a ten yard penalty, or something similar. Breaking these rules is fully encompassable within the game. These sorts of rules I call DEFEASIBLE rules. Language, as we shall see, has many characteristics in common with a rough-and-tumble game. Considering the circumstances in which it is used, it would be peculiar if it did not.

Indefeasible rules need no illustration; their existence is widely recognized. However, defeasible rules do need illustration. They are discussed more thoroughly in the next chapter so one example will suffice here:

> *When one says* I promise to do such and such *one is required, at that time, to intend to do that thing.*

This rule is not, anyway solely or mainly, a moral rule. One can see that it is fundamentally a semantic rule in this way. If people, all the time, said *I promise to do such and such* with no intention whatever of doing that thing, then it is not that they would all be immoral but that the idiom *I promise to* ... would mean something different from what it now means. However, the existence of this semantic rule does not imply that one speaks nonsensically when one says *I promise to meet you tomorrow* having no intention of doing so, i.e., breaking the rule does not vitiate the activity one is involved in. Breaking the rule is encompassed within the activity in just the way that being *off-side* in football is encompassed within the game; it involves consequences when it is detected. In the case of promising without intending, the consequences are moral censure, perhaps loss of trustworthiness in the eyes of others, and so on.[4]

It must be emphasized that breaking a defeasible rule is not the same as invoking the Over-riding Rule. When, in normal circumstances, one promises without intending the rule about promising and intending is not OBVIOUSLY broken (it is unlikely that the person to whom the promise is made realizes that the rule is being broken), so the conditions for the invocation of the Over-riding Rule are absent. Of course, one can perfectly well invoke the Over-riding Rule using the idiom *I promise to....* For instance, if someone promises to bring in a square circle before lunch he is, presumably, making a poor joke; he does so by invoking the Over-riding Rule.

To sum up: using language is a rule guided activity but this does not mean that breaking the rules immediately make one's utterances gibberish. There are two importantly different ways in which language rules can be broken without talking gibberish. The Over-riding Rule allows one to break any breakable rule under suitable circumstances (there is no problem over self-reference with the Over-riding Rule here: it is unbreakable in the way discussed at the beginning of the chapter). However, the circumstances under

[4] I have developed the notion of the semantic (logical) connection between such notions as promising and intending, asserting and believing, etc. at much greater length elsewhere. See "Logical Connection", *American Philosophical Quarterly* (January, 1967); "Entrenchment and Engagement", *Analysis* (March, 1967).

which it is permissible to invoke the Over-riding Rule are quite stringent. On the other hand, defeasible rules can also be broken without talking gibberish, though not usually without staining one's reputation.

There are, of course, more rules and more types of rule than those given here, both in language and outside it. However, these distinctions are all that are needed for my present undertaking.

5

SOME TYPES OF SEMANTIC RULES

In the last chapter an example of a certain type of semantic rule was given to illustrate the idea of a defeasible rule. This type of semantic rule is the most difficult. In this chapter I shall develop a more general theory of semantic rules, putting the type exemplified in the last chapter into its proper place.

It is worth mentioning, perhaps, that I am developing the notion of semantic rules before discussing syntactical rules, which is an unconventional approach to language theory, for this reason: linguistic theory has suffered in the past because some linguists have made practical mistakes in semantic theory while doing theoretical work in grammar and syntax. To clear up these errors it is necessary to offer some semantic theory here which, had these errors not been committed, would more conveniently have come in a later chapter. The cash value of this is seen in the next chapter which is concerned with the notion of a grammatically well formed sentence of a language as it appears (or is kept out of) the work of Noam Chomsky and C. C. Fries. A discussion of Chomsky's and Fries' grammatical theories comes in the following chapters.

I shall first define one technical term, OPEN SENTENCE, and discuss another pervasive concept, that of VERBAL DEFINITION.

An open sentence is either (a) a grammatically well formed sentence[1] which has had a variable placed for a word or a phrase in it, or (b) an open sentence under (a) above which has had a variable

---

[1] The concept of a GRAMMATICALLY WELL FORMED SENTENCE is discussed in the next chapter. As will be seen from that discussion, there is nothing improper or obscure about the use of the concept here without definition.

placed for a word or a phrase in it, this (b) rule being recursive (to say the (b) rule is recursive here is just to say that it can be reapplied as often as is necessary). To exemplify, from the grammatically well formed sentence *My car is red* we can form the open sentences *My car is A, My A is B, C is D* and so on. The variable need not, of course, be written with a literal: the first example given above could as well have been written: *My car is ....* The concept of an open sentence is allied to the notion of an ALLOWABLE SUBSTITUEND. Allowable substituends, in this context, are simply those values which the variable or variables shall, as a matter of stipulation, be allowed to take on. One speaks of an open sentence being INSTAN-TIATED when allowable substituends have been placed for the varia-bles. To take an example using all these different concepts: from the sentence *My car is red* we can form the open sentence *My car is A.* Let us suppose that it is specified that an allowable substituend for the variable is any word which, substitued for the variable, forms a grammatically well formed sentence; then *red, blue, yellow, old, fast, expensive,* etc. are all allowable substituends. *My car is old* would be one instantiation of the open sentence. The idea of an open sentence was first presented in a relatively formal way by Aristotle in the *Prior Analytics* and it is fair to say, I think, that no important theoretical work has been done since that time without making use of the notion.[2] It is completely fundamental to the theories discussed and presented in this monograph.

The concept of verbal definition is more complex than is usually realized. Let us first take a simpler notion. A word W is VERBALLY DEFINABLE when there is at least one value for the dot-variable in the open sentence *The word 'W' means ...* such that, when that value is substituted for the variable, the sentence formed expresses a true statement. That statement then gives a verbal definition of W. This gives a sufficient condition for a word being verbally definable and for the notion of verbal definition. However, it does not give a

---

[2] A possible exception is some work in philosophical theology. This comes about not because the work is intellectually bad but because the subject of the enquiry is only one thing (God) rather than a type of thing (nouns, electrons, numbers).

necessary condition, for there are many variations on the open sentences which can be used to give a verbal definition. Trivially, the open sentence, *The word 'W' is defined as follows*: ... would do as well. Less trivially, if the adjective *A* can only be used to modify the noun *N*, and if *N* is verbally definable in the way given above and the phrase *A N* is verbally definable in the way given above, then we want to say that, as a consequence, *A* is verbally definable. There are many further ramifications possible but we need not go into them here. Essentially giving a verbal definition of a word *W* involves specifying a translation procedure such that a sentence containing *W* can be translated into another sentence or other sentences which do not contain *W*.

The ideal way to give the meaning of a word, or so we tend to feel, is to give a verbal definition of it. Thus if, as is the case, we can say that the word *autobiography* means the story of at least part of a person's life told by himself we feel we have fulfilled the demand to give the meaning of the word *autobiography* impeccably. However, it is easy to see that the notion of verbal definition as such is not the foundation of semantic theory: Take the English language with vocabulary V_0. Put V_0 in serial order. Working down the series, eliminate the first verbally definable word. This forms a new vocabulary V_1. Proceed identically with V_1. Continue until a vocabulary V_n is achieved such that no word is verbally definable. Clearly V_n is not empty, for there would have been no words in which to define the last word. In the language associated with V_n it is the case that (a) anything which can be said in English can be said in it, and (b) no word is verbally definable. Thus the language associated with the vocabulary V_n is, in important respects, equivalent to English: it has a truncated vocabulary but it is hardly a truncated language.[3] The crucial point about the language associated with V_n is the combination of the two properties that it is, in important respects, equivalent to English and that no word in it is verbally

---

[3] The language associated with the vocabulary V_n would, doubtless, be less expressive than English and in it nothing could be said about the vocabulary items of V_0 which are not also vocabulary items of V_n. In all other respects, the languages would be equivalent.

definable. Thus verbal definition cannot be the foundation, or anyway the entire content of, semantic theory. However, a broadened notion, of which verbal definition is a special case, is very important in semantic theory. This is outlined below.

When verbal definition of a word can be given, we can see the word as surrounded by a set of entailment relations of this general type:[4]

> *X is an autobiography* entails *X is the story of at least part of a person's life.*

(The statement of this entailment relations gives, of course, a semantic rule.) A set of these entailment relations define the word (if it is definable): to say a word is verbally definable is to say that there are a set of entailment relations which give all the semantic rules which govern its correct use. As shown above, not all words in a language need be verbally definable, but that does not amount to saying that a word which is not verbally definable is involved in no such entailment relations as these. Indeed, this clearly need not be the case. The word *red* is not verbally definable in any interesting way (it does not define *red* to say something about the wave length

---

[4] The philosophical term ENTAILMENT is probably well enough understood among linguists to need no special definition. However, for the sake of completeness, I give the definition here; it is, unfortunately, a little complex. When p and q are sentences, then

> p ENTAILS q

if and only if p expressing a true statement guarantees (requires) that q shall express a true statement. When s and r are open sentences and where every variable which appears in r also appears in s, then

> s ENTAILS r

if and only if, for every substitution for the variables in s which turns s into a sentence which expresses a true statement, the same substitution for the same variables in r turns r into a sentence which expresses a statement which is true and whose truth is guaranteed (required) by the truth of the statement generated from s. (It is possible to produce a definition of ENTAILMENT between open sentences s and r where it is not required that every variable which appears in r also appears in s, but it is not necessary for my present purposes).

An additional note for philosophers: it will be noticed that these definitions avoid the paradoxes of material and strict implication and that ENTAILMENT as I have defined it is therefore suitable for use in semantic theory. See further my "Logical Connection", *American Philosophical Quarterly* (1967).

of light: that is a scientific theory about light). However, in spite of being indefinable, the following is true:

X is red entails *X is coloured.*

Such statements of entailment relations are semantic rules for the use of the word concerned.

It is crucial to see how important such rules are for the meaning of a word and that they are, or can be, independent of particular applications of the word. The point is most easily seen with an artificial example. Philosophers have, in the past, often been interested in talking about material objects. The word *material object* was given meaning (insofar as it was given meaning) by giving examples of its correct application. Material objects, we were told, are things like chairs, tables, pictures, books, flowers, pens, cigarettes (A. J. Ayer). But this leaves the notion of a material object completely obscure. Suppose a cigarette is cut in half. We then have two halves of one cigarette, and the inside is visible; but do we now have two material objects, whose insides we can never see, or one material object cut in half? It does not matter what answer is given to that question: the point is that it must be answered for the term to be meaningful in the context in which it was used and the answer would be a logical or semantic rule.

In the previous chapter, two types of rule were delineated: what I called defeasible and indefeasible rules. Semantic rules are of both these types. Earlier in this chapter, examples of indefeasible semantic rules are given expressed in entailment relations; for instance, the rule

X is red entails *X is coloured,*

was given. In the previous chapter, the example of a defeasible semantic rule given was as follows:

When one says I promise to do such and such *one is required, at that time, to intend to do that thing.*

This is a poor way to express such a rule, if for no other reason than it looks like a moral rule. A better way to express such a rule is by using a relational word analogous to *entailment*: I use the word *engagement* (the corresponding verb being *engage*); the phonological similarities between ENGAGEMENT and ENTAILMENT are, of course, deliberate. We can then write the rule about promising and intending as follows:

> *A says 'I promise to X' engages A intends to do X.*

However, the term ENGAGEMENT is still undefined. I do not propose to give a full definition of the term because doing so is an extremely long and complex matter and unnecessary for what is needed here.[5] For our present purposes, the following fairly loose definition will do: When s and r are open sentences and when every variable which appears in r also appears in s, then

> *s* engages *r*

if and only if, under ideal and non-frivolous circumstances of language use (mainly where no one is trying to deceive anyone else), for every substitution for the variables in s which turns s into a sentence which expresses a true statement, the same substitution for the same variables in r turns r into a sentence which expresses a statement which is true and whose truth is guaranteed by the truth of the statement generated from s.[6]

Semantic rules not expressible in terms of entailment relations but expressible in terms of engagement relations are very common in the language. Some of them have to do with the (semantic) function of certain types of utterance and types of sentence,[7] and others to do with the meanings of, most obviously, common nouns. Here are some examples (allowable substituends for 'A' are people's names or referred pronouns, for 'S' sentences which are statemental in form, for 'X' any word which leaves the sentence grammatically well formed):

[5] I have endeavoured to give a completely precise definition in my "Entrenchment and Engagement", *Analysis* (1967).

[6] It is possible to produce a definition of ENGAGEMENT in these terms between open sentences s and r where it is not required that every variable which appears in r also appears in s, but it is not necessary for my present purposes.

[7] So far as I know, this is the first attempt in semantic theory to get at the semantic content of the functions of utterances on sentences. Cf. Chomsky, *Aspects of the Theory of Syntax*, p. 163.

On the functions of types of utterance and types of sentences:

1. A says 'S' *engages* A believes that S.
2. A asks for X *engages* A wants X.
3. A wants X *engages* A will try to get X.

On the meanings of nouns:

4. X is a rabbit *engages* X has long ears.
5. X is a man *engages* X breathes.
6. X is an emerald *engages* X is green.

To be in command of the meanings of words and sentences in any language it is necessary to be in command of both entailment and engagement rules. They are very different types of rule. I point out some of these differences in Appendix III, sections #7 and #8. For the present it is sufficient to notice this: that entailment rules give necessary conditions for the CORRECT use of a word, where engagement rules give necessary conditions for what we might call the HAPPY use of a word. HAPPINESS and CORRECTNESS differ markedly for there is nothing linguistically incorrect about many unhappy uses of words. For instance, many unhappy uses of words are deceptive in some way (e.g., promising without intending to perform, saying what one does not believe). But their being deceptive depends on their making perfectly good sense, i.e., breaking no entailment rules except, perhaps, by invoking the Over-riding Rule. We do not speak deceptively when we speak gibberish. As a consequence, an inspection of long enough passages of correct English should make it possible to discover the entailment rules (actual ways to do this are discussed in Chapter 11). However, to discover the engagement rules it is presumably necessary to inspect more than just well formed sentences of the language; it would seem to be a good guess that one must also understand something of the forms of social behaviour.[8] There may be a way round this, as I suggest

---

[8] Wittgenstein made this point some years ago when he pointed out that imagining a language involved imagining, not just a code, but a form of life. This part of Wittgenstein's work has been largely ignored by philosophers of language, even those avowedly influenced by him (see *Philosophical Investigations*, Section 32 and ff.).

in Chapter 11, but I do not yet see what it is with any clarity.

What is important for my present purposes is to note two things: that both entailment and engagement rules are necessary for an adequate semantic theory but that there seems to be no obvious way to detect engagement rules mechanically. It is the entailment rules, or anyway some of them, which the computer program discussed in the last chapter is designed to detect.

6

GRAMMATICALLY WELL FORMED SENTENCES

Let us return for a moment to the conclusion of the first argument in the last chapter. The argument showed that it is possible to have a language which is, to all intents and purposes, equivalent to English and where no word whatever is definable. It follows that verbal definition as such need not be the basis of meaningfulness in words. More specifically, it follows that to say a word cannot be verbally defined is not in any sense to say that the word has no meaning or is vague; it may of course be vague or meaningless, but lack of any verbal definition is not a reason for saying it is so. This last point is important and frequently overlooked. In fact, there is no difference in vagueness between verbally definable words and words which cannot be verbally defined because of being or not being verbally definable. That is, verbally definable words must all, at some remove, be defined in terms of words which cannot be verbally defined; therefore these words, in spite of being definable, have all the vagueness of indefinable words. To say of a word that it is vague is to assess it along a completely different dimension than the dimension of verbally definable or not verbally definable.[1]

This leaves the problems of how a word which cannot be verbally defined can be meaningful and how its meaning can be learned (this is really two aspects of the same problem). To try to solve this problem here would be off my main line, quite apart from the fact that its general solution is certainly going to be very long and com-

---

[1] This was illustrated earlier. The notion of A WORD in an indo-european language, though not definable, is not as vague as the notion of a morpheme, which is definable.

plex. I shall therefore say only four things about it: (a) The solution does not lie in simply saying such words are 'ostensively' defined[2] partly because (b) the nature of ostensive definition is not at present well understood and what is usually said about it is radically muddled,[3] and partly because (c) even with those words which can only be taught by giving an ostensive definition (whatever that may be), this, though a necessary condition of their being taught, is not a sufficient condition; their meaning also requires explanation in terms of the sorts of semantic rules discussed in the last chapter.[4] Finally, (d) however much there are theoretical problems in this area, it is quite certain that we do learn to use words which are not verbally definable entirely successfully, and with all the precision the more precise words of our language have; that fact is all that is needed for the present study.

We have, then, reached this point: some words are verbally definable and some are not; whether or not a word is verbally definable is not itself a factor in whether the word's meaning can be learned, in whether it is vague or not, precise or not, etc. Failing to realize these points led both Chomsky and Fries (as well as many other linguists) into unnecessary difficulties over the concept of a grammatically well formed sentence. Because they could not define the term they felt that it was necessarily woolly and imprecise. As a consequence Fries rejects the whole concept out of hand and refuses to use it at all, while Chomsky speaks of using it in the most apologetic tone of voice. Consider the following quotation from *Syntactic Structures*: "For the purposes of this discussion ... suppose we assume intuitive knowledge of the grammatical sentences of English ..." He is unhappy about having made this assumption and tries to excuse himself: "Notice that in order to set the aims of grammar significantly it is sufficient to assume a partial knowledge of sentences and non-sentences. That is, we may assume for this

---

[2] Wheatley, "How To Give a Word a Meaning", *Theoria* (1964).

[3] Wheatley, "Like", *Proceedings of the Aristotelian Society* (1961-62).

[4] Wittgenstein, *Philosophical Investigations*, Sections 28 to 43. "Ostensive definition explains the use — the meaning — of the word [only] when the overall role of the word in language is clear" (Section 30). The inserted *only* is mine and is substantial. Its justification, however, is not short.

discussion that certain sequences of phonemes are definitely sentences, and that certain other sequences are definitely non-sentences" (pp. 13-14). But Chomsky's diffidence here is misplaced and Fries was quite wrong in his reasons for rejecting the concept of a sentence wholly. It is important to see why.

A grammatically well formed sentence of English is a sentence which educated native speakers of the language recognize as being grammatically well formed. They need not do so by using the predicate *is a grammatically well formed sentence of the language,* of course, but there are less formal and completely adequate idioms which get at exactly the concept that grammarians are after. What happens is that sentences are uttered (written) all the time and most go uncriticised and understood; some, however, are said to be *bad English, bad grammar, wrongly formed,* and so on. This locates the difference between grammatically well formed sentences and other strings of words.[5] I shall now justify this claim.

To repeat what was claimed above: whether or not a word is verbally definable is not itself a factor in whether the word's meaning can be learned, in whether it is vague or not, precise or not, etc. Thus the only reason for verbally defining a word (except, perhaps, for the intrinsic interest of the task) is that, undefined, there is no good way to decide when it should be used and when it should not, when it is applicable and when it is not applicable. Thus the demand that a word needs verbal definition must have behind it an empirical claim that there is difficulty about applying it or using it correctly. This claim is not justified for the notion of being a grammatically well formed sentence. It is a fact that educated native speakers of a language have no difficulty in recognizing what is and what is not a grammatically well formed sentence of that language in most instances.[6] It has been said, as if it were somehow disgraceful, that

---

[5]   This is not, of course, a definition of GRAMMATICALLY WELL FORMED SENTENCE any more than saying that what is red is what educated native speakers of English call red defines the word *red.*

[6]   The difficulties which Fries creates for himself over this point are almost unbelievable. He supposes, for instance, that the fact that a group of teachers punctuated a given passage of prose differently, as regards their use of periods, is evidence that they do not know a sentence when they see one. But this is

this is a very convenient fact about language. But that it is a fact is not something which just (conveniently enough) happens to be the case. If learning a language did not involve learning to recognize grammatically well formed sentences of that language, the language would have no grammar. A 'language' without a grammar would not be a language. That there is so very little difficulty about educated native speakers of most languages agreeing on what is a grammatically well formed sentence over such a very wide area is doubtless a contingent fact. That there should be wide agreement over a large range of cases is, however, a necessary condition of having a language at all. It must be emphasized that this is a completely compulsive logical argument; not a matter of opinion or supposition.

Thus the concept of a grammatically well formed sentence is a completely firm element in any grammatical theory we build. It is not a notion which needs defining at all, except insofar as trying to uncover the grammar of a language is the endeavor to define a grammatically well formed sentence of that language.

The argument of this chapter is completely central to my whole endeavor in this monograph. It is therefore worth repeating its main points.

1. Not every word in any language is verbally definable. In fact, we can construct a language which, to all intents and purposes, is equivalent to any given language and has no definable words.

2. Words which are verbally definable are not, for that reason, more precise or better understood than indefinable words.

3. Therefore the search for a definition of a word is only justifiable on grounds of precision where there are grounds, other than its not being verbally definable, to suppose it imprecise or unintelligible.

---

absurd. That they divided the passage into sentences differently matters not at all (it is a well known stylistic device to divide sentences in apposition with a colon or a semi-colon; and Fries' passage lends itself to this sort of treatment). What would have been important is if Fries' teachers had divided the passage into non-sentences while claiming that they were dividing it into sentences. I do not imagine they did so (Fries offers us no information on this point) but if they did they were not competent to teach English.

4. There are no such grounds with the concept of a grammatically well formed sentence.

5. Therefore the concept of a grammatically well formed sentence is entirely suitable as a founding concept in grammatical theory.

7

THE TRANSFORMATIONAL APPROACH TO GRAMMAR

Grammar is the study of and the search for the rules for generating possible utterances and for forming morphological variants on the vocabulary items of a language. The rules for forming morphological variants are relatively well understood, considered in isolation from the rules for utterance formation; that is, we know and can state, e.g., the rules for forming the plurals of English nouns. What is not so well understood are the rules for utterance formation.

The best known attempt to explicate these rules today is the work on transformational or generative grammar, usually associated with the name of Noam Chomsky and deriving from the work of Zellig Harris. The basic idea behind a transformational grammar is this: that the rules for generating possible utterances (well formed sentences) constitute the grammar or syntax of a language. A correct grammar is one which states a set of recursive rules such that repeated application of these rules to certain basic sentence forms produces all and only well formed sentences of the language. If the method of derivation for any one sentence is unique (which it is the aim of the theory that it should be) the derivation provides an analysis (a PHRASE STRUCTURE ANALYSIS) of the sentence.

It is worthwhile exemplifying this in more detail. Consider such a simple sentence form as

$$N + V,$$

where N = noun and V = verb. It is exemplified by such simple sentences as *John eats* or *Susan cries*. A whole set of sentences can be generated by substituting different nouns for N and different verbs for V. If we use the symbolism: S = sentence and '→' for *may be rewritten as*, we can write this sentence form as a rule, as follows:

R1   S → N + V

Let us suppose that we have, in addition, the following recursive rules, where A = adjective, NP = noun phrase, VP = verb phrase:

R2   V → VP
R3   N → NP
R4   NP → *the* + N
R5   NP → *to* + VP
R6   NP → *that* + S
R7   VP → V + A

giving us a total of seven rules. It should be noticed that these rules are of the very simplest type and any adequate grammar of English will require more complicated rules. For instance, rules of the type,

XAY → XBY.

That is, rules which specify that when the part of speech A appears in the context where X is to the left of it and Y to the right of it, then B may be written for A.

Even for these six simple rules, sentences of some complexity may be generated very freely. Here is a sample derivation. The rules used in making each derivation appear to the right of each line in brackets.

S → N + V   (R1)
N + V → NP + VP   (R2&3)
NP + VP → *to* + VP + VP   (R5)

which gives a sentence form of which *To err is human* is an exemplification. Alternatively, to show the recursive nature of these rules, we can make the following derivation[1] (there is no necessity to write what appears to the left of the arrow except in the first line):

[1]   This example is adapted from a paper of Chomsky's: "A Transformational Approach to Syntax" from the *Proceedings of the Third Texas Conference on Problems of Linguistic Analysis of English* (1962).

$$S \rightarrow N + V \qquad\qquad\qquad\qquad\qquad\qquad (R1)$$
$$\rightarrow NP + VP \qquad\qquad\qquad\qquad\qquad (R2\&3)$$
$$\rightarrow (that + S) + VP \qquad\qquad\qquad\qquad (R6)$$
$$\rightarrow (that + (N + V)) + VP \qquad\qquad\qquad (R1)$$
$$\rightarrow (that + (NP + V)) + VP \qquad\qquad\quad (R3)$$
$$\rightarrow (that + ((the + N) + V)) + VP \qquad\quad (R4)$$
$$\rightarrow (that + ((the + N) + V)) + (V + A) \qquad (R7)$$

which gives a sentence of the form of which *That the man came was unfortunate* is an exemplification. From this derivation, an (ideally unique) phrase structure analysis of the sentence can be given. This may be done by means of brackets (as I have done partially above) but it is easier to see what is involved with the more graphic tree diagram. It is as follows:

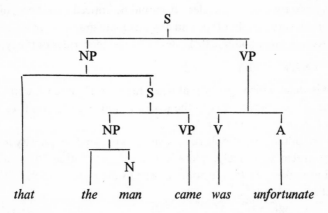

Such a diagram (a phrase structure diagram) gives what Chomksy calls the surface structure of the sentence *That the man came was unfortunate*.

This approach to grammar has two notable disadvantages, one of which is too little emphasized by transformational grammarians and the other of which is largely ignored.

(1) In so far as transformational grammar is seen as a way of generating sentences, rather than sentence forms, it has to be combined with a semantic theory which is a great deal more sophisti-

cated than anything so far envisaged. Take this simple sentence form:

$$N + V.$$

It is a possible sentence form of English in the sense that a great many possible sentences have this form. But it is not a sentence form of English if by this is meant that substitution of any noun for N and any verb for V will produce an utterance of English. For instance, *Mary rains*, outside very special contexts, just means nothing. Transformational grammarians are aware of this problem. They take account of it in two ways: (a) by distinguishing between what is nonsensical because grammatically ill-formed, and what is nonsensical for semantic reasons while being grammatically well formed; (b) by asserting, what may well be correct, that no grammatically well formed sentence is meaningless in this sense: that in certain (doubtless sometimes very special) contexts and to perform certain (doubtless very special) jobs, any grammatically well formed sentence is meaningful. Take the example (from Russell) of *Saturday's in bed*. This need not be meaningless or nonsensical. It makes perfectly good sense to say *Friday night is drunk, Saturday's in bed, Sunday's at church and Monday's back at the old grind again*. Doubtless ingenuity could provide Chomsky's example of *Colourless green ideas sleep furiously* with a similar use. These answers would be adequate, if also spurs to further work on the join between syntax and semantics, did they not lead to the second difficulty.

(2) Transformational grammar uses, as building blocks, the traditional parts of speech, i.e., nouns, verbs, adjectives, and so on. However, the classification of parts of speech in English is, as is well known, largely incoherent. To take the most striking example, NOUN and ADJECTIVE are defined across categories. That is, a noun is defined as the name of a person, place or thing; this is a semantic definition (and incorrect: the boy's name is *Michael* not *boy*). An adjective is defined as a word which modifies a noun or a pronoun; this is a functional definition (it also is incorrect: what an adjective modifies is the set to which the noun, so qualified, may be correctly applied). Ignoring the straight errors (which are correctable) and the difference in type between the definitions, they just do not fit

the facts of language. In *his hat*, *his* is not usually considered to be an adjective, nor is *boy's* in *the boy's dog*; similarly, *stone* in *stone cold coffee* is not considered to be an adverb. The same thing applies in reverse: in *That's the blue I want*, *blue*, though one would tend to say it here fulfills the function of a noun, fits the definition of neither a noun nor an adjective. Similarly, in *Five is a prime number*, *five* has a noun position though it is usually classified as an adjective.

This affects work in transformational grammar in two ways. First, one must realize that the phrase structure analyses which use or embody the traditional parts of speech without question are nowhere near as clear as they appear to be. Secondly, by taking less central cases of the traditional parts of speech than those usually considered, the sentence forms produced are less obviously forms of grammatically correct (if sometimes odd) sentences. Consider the sentence form:

$$(The + (A + N)) + V + A).$$

This form instantiates into *The tall boy is running*, which is grammatically well formed and in all other respects unexceptionable. However, it also instantiates into *The five Mary is green* or, with a suitable neologistic plural for *Mary*, *The five Marys are green*. Equally, it instantiates into *The this boy is five*.[2] To say these sentences are grammatically well formed if, perhaps, meaningless (like *Colourless green ideas sleep furiously*) is to sacrifice the facts to save the theory.[3]

---

[2] Or is *this* a pronoun? Most dictionaries list it as both a pronoun and an adjective. Presumably it is to be a pronoun in such sentences as *This is red* and an adjective in *This hat is red*. I wonder whether lexicographers would also call it an adverb if the sentence *This red is the one I want* were brought to their attention. But these distinctions are bogus. If we take the traditional definitions of parts of speech seriously at all, *this* must be an adjective which, like many adjectives in the traditional classification, can sometimes occupy a noun (pronoun) position in a sentence. But that, in turn, is a reason for not taking the traditional classification seriously: *this* is not of a type with *red*.

[3] There is a new classification of parts of speech assumed, though never made explicit, in the majority of work on transformational grammar. Thus *that*, *to*, [4]*he*, etc., get used in recursive rules where this would seem unneccessary: all that should be required is to put in the appropriate part of speech. But, as we all know, that would not work at all.

In fact, the situation is worse than this. The whole movement of transformational grammar is to produce sentence forms which instantiate into grammatically well formed sentences of the language. But I have never seen work by transformational grammarians where there is any serious attempt to investigate the borderline cases. If this had been done it surely would have become obvious that transformational theory has to be allied to a new classification of words of English (or any language).

None of this is seriously against transformational grammar as such; in fact, I have little doubt that some form of transformational grammar is correct. That the rules for any adequate grammar for a non-primitive language must be recursive is surely provable by a transcendental argument. Equally, that the rules should be of the general form Chomsky and others envisage seems, with one point of difficulty, to be undoubtedly correct. The point of difficulty, that discussed above, is that the traditional grammatical classifications do not seem suitable to be the TERMS in the rules, anyway not without radical modification. Equally, but less importantly, if we are interested in such things as machine translation, which is a highly practical activity, something more will have to be done in clarifying the difference between well formed sentences which have no obvious meaning (even if we can think up highly odd contexts where they would make sense), and sheer grammatical and semantic nonsense.

8

CLASSIFYING PARTS OF SPEECH

The most interesting current attempt to classify the parts of speech is that given by C. C. Fries, most notably in *The Structure of English*. He makes this attempt using two basic notions: the idea of a SENTENCE FRAME and that of STRUCTURAL MEANING.

The idea of a sentence frame in Fries' work is ambiguous, though not importantly so. The basic notion is this: take an open sentence of English[1] and see what are allowable substituends for the variable or variables (in all his detailed work he uses single-variable open sentences). The ambiguity arises in this way: Fries never indicates unambiguously whether it is the sentence from which the open sentence is generated or the open sentence itself which is the frame.[2] In what follows, I shall use OPEN SENTENCE and SENTENCE rather than FRAME for the sake of accuracy. I do not think this leads to a misrepresentation of Fries' position.

Fries' notion of an allowable substituend in an open sentence is more difficult. He says, in effect, that an allowable substituend is one which leaves unaltered the STRUCTURAL MEANING of the sentence from which the open sentence was generated. Clearly this puts great weight on the notion of structural meaning. Here is an

[1] Fries, as we have seen, rejects the notion of a sentence; instead he prefers to speak in terms of MINIMUM FREE UTTERANCES. As we have seen, his reasons for rejecting the notion of a sentence were inadequate. But, in any case, all the minimum free utterances used by Fries in creating frames are recognizably sentences so the change is only theoretical. I shall continue to talk of sentences here. It does not, I think, introduce inaccuracies in my representation of Fries.
[2] On p. 70 he refers to *Did X and Y in the Z* as a frame; on p. 75 he refers to *The concert was good* as a frame. However, what he means is always clear in context, which is the reason the ambiguity is unimportant.

extended quotation from Fries giving his description of that concept:

Let us begin ... with the sentence ..., *the man gave the boy the money.* First of all, we need to distinguish sharply at least two kinds of meaning in the total meaning of this utterance. There are, for example, the meanings of the separate words as the dictionary would record them — the lexical meanings. The dictionary would tell us something of the kinds of creatures referred to by the words *man* and *boy*; it would tell us the sort of thing the word *money* represents; and it would tell us the kind of action indicated by the word *gave*. Beyond these meanings the dictionary does not go. And yet we get from this sentence a whole range of meanings not expressed in the lexical records of the words themselves. We are told, for example, that the "man" performed the action, not the "boy"; and we are told that only one man and only one boy are involved; we are told that the action has already taken place, it is not something in process, not something planned for the future; the information is given to us as a statement of fact, not something that is questioned, nor something which is requested. Such meanings constitute what we shall call the STRUCTURAL MEANINGS of the sentence. The total linguistic meaning of any utterance consists of the lexical meanings of the separate words plus such structural meanings. How, then, are these structural meanings conveyed in English from the speaker to the hearer? Structural meanings are not just vague matters of the context, so-called; they are fundamental and necessary meanings in every utterance and are signalled by specific and definite devices. It is the devices that signal structural meanings which constitute the grammar of a language. The grammar of a language consists of the devices that signal structural meanings (p. 55-56).

The classification of parts of speech then proceeds as follows: Fries selected a sentence and formed an open sentence by placing a variable for one word in it. A possible substituend for the variable was a word which left unaltered the structural meaning of the sentence from which the open sentence was generated. The class of allowable substituends for any one open sentence was then said to be some one part of speech. It is of great importance for his theory that he specifies that a possible substituend is not one which produces a grammatically well formed sentence but one which produces a sentence whose structural meaning is identical to the structural meaning of the original sentence.

What Fries never appreciates is that the very vague and diffuse description he gives of structural meaning entirely vitiates his enterprise. He realises the notion is not well defined, for he writes "It was not necessary for us to define the structural meaning ...; we had simply to make certain whether, with each substitution, the structural meaning was the same as that of our first example or different from it" (p. 74). But, if the notion of structural meaning is not well defined, how does he propose to make certain (even make a good guess) that structural meaning remains unchanged? This is not an academic worry which does not arise in practice; it arises all the time. For instance, in the sentence,

The boy was kicking the chair,

can *on* be substituted for *kicking* without change in structural meaning? There is nothing whatever in Fries' description of structural meaning which gives the smallest hint as to what the answer is.

I do not doubt that any procedure for generating a grammar which consists in forming putative sentences by some mechanical procedure and then deciding whether they are grammatical, identical in structural meaning, or what have you, is going to suffer from arbitrariness through quite a broad band of cases. This does not rule out such a procedure, because some degree of arbitrariness in discussing the grammar of a highly expressive language is doubtless inevitable. However, to face the necessity of some degree of arbitrariness is no excuse for not always working to eliminate it. Furthermore, though Fries has a stance which would indicate that he was seeking objectivity, his actual program completely fails to catch it. His proposed procedure does not have just some degree of arbitrariness: it completely lacks even a putative decision procedure to save it from total arbitrariness.

One would suppose that this difficulty could be overcome by better defining the notion of structural meaning. However, it seems unlikely that this can be done, anyway if one takes Fries' position on structural meaning seriously. That is, in the last two sentences of the passage quoted, Fries virtually identifies grammar with structural meaning. In this he would appear to be right. This amounts to saying that to define STRUCTURAL MEANING well we must give the grammar of the language involved. But this is self-defeating; structural meaning was to be used as a tool in investigating the grammar of a language. Yet it can only be an effective tool when the problem it is designed to solve is already solved. Therefore working on a better definition of structural meaning is no solution to Fries' problem.

However, I wish to ignore this difficulty with the notion of structural meaning for a moment, i.e., assume something can be done to resuscitate the notion of structural meaning, so I may discuss two further problems in Fries' method of classification. The point of doing so becomes apparent in the next chapter.

The first difficulty is this: what grammatical type a word falls into, under Fries' method of classification, depends on the original choice of sentences to turn into open sentences. For instance, Fries classifies *and* and *on* as different parts of speech. Using the open sentences (Frames) he uses, this is correct. But it is easy to make up an open sentence where this would not be the case. Consider the open sentence

Boys ———— *horses are dangerous.*

Here both *and* and *on* are substitutable. Whether or not Fries would wish to say that the structural meaning had changed I do not know. If he wished to say it has changed, and that therefore this possibility of substitution gives no evidence that *and* and *on* are the same part of speech, then the notion of CHANGE OF STRUCTURAL MEANING would transparently have become a device for getting the results he wants.

The second problem is this: Fries says explicitly that when words are classified by his method they are classified "only in the particular lexical meaning" they have in the sentence under consideration (p. 75). He has this sort of situation in mind. A word in a definite utterance picks up what it actually means there in part from context. For instance, consider the sentence

He stopped the car because the light was against him.

Light here means *traffic light*. Fries wants to say that, when a word is classified by his method, it must be considered to be classified in the full-fledged meaning it has in the sentence used to classify it. Thus we must not be surprised if the same word is classified in more than one way.

These two difficulties are worth stating just so we can see that they are not particularly important, though they require revision of theory. That our classification of parts of speech depends on the particular instruments we use in classification is not surprising. But it does require that we pick the instruments (the sentences, Frames, in this case) with great care to get just the classification which we want and which is most useful. Fries' mistake here is only that he supposes (or appears to) that any old Frame will do for classificatory purposes. This is not the case. A great deal of research could, and should, go into picking the right Frames.[3]

The second difficulty is similar. Fries is aware of it, and says so in a footnote. After a further *caveat*, also in a footnote, he forgets all about it and we get long lists of words of certain grammatical types; many of them patently of more than one grammatical type according to Fries' method of classification. This was careless of him, but the actual problem, when tackled head-on, is not very serious. At least one way round it, a way taken in a cumbersome form now in the conventional classification of words into parts of speech, is to note that a word can be of more than one grammatical type. For instance *run* can be either a noun or a verb, and the dictionary notes this fact. A better way, it would seem to me, would be to invent a new grammatical category (called NERBS, perhaps) which contains those words of English which are both nouns and verbs. In English, this constitutes a large and important class of words which it would be well worth our while to isolate.

Finally, we should notice this: that these last two difficulties of Fries' system of classification, though not destructive of the essentials of that system, have other problems associated with them. Most obviously, to use the methods of generative grammarians, we

[3] Fries uses as his first frame the first sentence he recorded in the series of telephone conversations he used as data. He gives no indication whether his picking the first sentence was deliberately random or whether the first sentence was in fact best suited to his classificatory scheme.

must have more stable classification of parts of speech than we are going to get out of a classificatory scheme such as Fries'.

A further point in Fries' work is worth noticing before proceeding. Fries himself was part of the movement which demanded that grammar should cease to be normative and should become, instead, descriptive. This was a reaction against past work in grammar where the emphasis was on insisting (unsuccessfully) that language-use should conform to certain past models. This reaction, in turn, gave rise to the idea that it is the spoken language rather than the written language which is somehow the most fundamental aspect of language-use and that it should, therefore, be the primary area for analysis. As a consequence, Fries used as data recorded telephone conversations.

The position that present language-use should conform to past models is, of course, ridiculous. Equally, there is no doubt that the foundation of all language is speech. However, it is doubtful whether the spoken language is a better subject for analysis than the written language. When we speak, we often do so to people we know well. Our shared background, tricks of intonation and gesture, references to private jokes and so on play a large part in the communicative function of our utterances. More importantly, we often do not finish sentences because how they would be finished is obvious. To put it another way, we cannot get at how we communicate by seeing how we actually talk because there is far more to communication when we talk than uttering certain words in a certain order. Luckily, however, not all talk is personal and semi-private in this way. We have no difficulty in communicating with a wider audience than our intimate friends and where the facilities of intonation, gesture, and so on are denied us. Crassly put, we can all write for publication and we do so, not in a semi-private idiom, but in the *lingua franca* of the English speaking community. It is this *lingua franca* which is the English language and which should concern us if we are interested in English rather than a local dialect of English. I must insist, therefore, that analysing the written word must be our concern, both because it is the *lingua franca* and because all that is said (what Fries called TOTAL MEANING) is in the sentences rather than in gestures or private and personal references. As will be seen, I favour for analysis the sort of writing found in (the more sober) newspapers.[4]

---

[4] Not only because it fulfills the sorts of conditions I have been discussing. It must be remembered that I am interested in analysing the language mechanically by computer. To do so requires that many grammatically well formed sentences are available for mechanical inspection. Several newspapers today are set by computers, which involves punching the text on to paper-tape. This punched tape is suitable input for a computer. The tape, which is a mere waste product once the newspaper is printed, would provide ideal and cheap data-input for such an analysis program.

9

MECHANICAL CLASSIFICATION OF PARTS
OF SPEECH

We have seen in the last chapter how Fries' classificatory procedure does not work. I now want to consider what lay behind his method and see whether it can be rebuilt.

Fries clearly wanted a classificatory technique which would be objective, rule governed, and useful. Furthermore, there seems little doubt that, so far as possible, he wanted to have a scheme where the grammatical classification of a word would be at least as stable as it now is. He failed, at least partially, in all these aims. I suspect that he failed only because he was not sufficiently iconoclastic in his approach to conventional grammar, though his advertised aim was to be totally iconoclastic.

The notion of structural meaning must be rejected as a basic, intuitively obvious, concept (it can perhaps be revived, but it must itself be based on other concepts). Detailed reasons for rejecting it were given in the last chapter but the real reason is simply this: that the concept of structural meaning has built into it most of the old grammar. What is needed is the very much more objective and basic notion of a grammatically well formed sentence.

What I propose to do now, then, is see what can be made out of a Friesian classificatory scheme by substituting the notion of GRAMMATICALLY WELL FORMED SENTENCE for SAMENESS OF STRUCTURAL MEANING. That is, I shall attempt to classify parts of speech by taking open sentences with only one variable and having, as allowable substituends for the variable, any word which, when substituted for the variable, gives a grammatically well formed sentence of the language. If every allowable substituend for a given variable is said to be the same part of speech, it is obvious that the difficulties discussed in the last chapter, other than those over the notion of **structural** meaning, will arise in an exacerbated form. That is, how words are classified will depend on what open sentences are used and the words will only be grammatically typed in the particular meaning they have when substituted into the particular open sentences used in the particular place which the variable now occupies. However, as we saw in that chapter, these are not totally vitiating difficulties.

The fundamental difficulty, baldly put, is this: too many words which, intuitively, are of radically different type will be classed in the same grammatical category. Take the famous passage of rhyming open sentences quoted from Lewis Carroll by Fries,

> Twas brillig, and the slithy toves
>   Did gyre and gimble in the wabe
> All mimsey were the borogroves
>   And the mome raths outgrabe ...

The first variable (*brillig*) will take a number of substitutions which keep the first sentence grammatically well formed. For instance, it will take words of the type *brilliant*, *Noon*, *water* and *Bill Sykes*. Though a classificatory scheme which grouped all these words together as an over-type might have advantages for certain purposes, it certainly would not do for a Chomskyesque generative grammar. However, there is no need to take an open sentence where, as we can well see, the over-type generated will be so very broad; nor need we use just one open sentence.

The reason *brillig* takes so many substitutions is that what can follow the verb *to be* is notoriously extremely various. However, suppose we take the open sentence

> The ———— boy walked to the bus-stop.

What will go for the variable, *salva grammaticale*,[1] is more or less limited to adjectives. Granted we will get, as adjectives, things

---

[1]   I apologize for using the Latin tag *salva grammaticale*. My excuse is that it is less barbarous than PRESERVING GRAMMATICALNESS, which was the only reasonably short alternative.

which behave as adjectives, like participles of verbs, and will not get all (conventional) adjectives, e.g., we will not get numbers over *one*. This however is of no importance at all. The present conventional classificatory scheme is arbitrary in many areas and we now need new ways to classify. If we did classify together all parts of speech which could go for the variable in this open sentence, *salva grammaticale*, we would have an entirely viable classification. Similarly, if we take the open sentence

———— *fat boy walked to the bus-stop*

possible substituends for the variable, *salva grammaticale*, would give a viable classification, though it would be an unconventional one. That is, *a*, and *the* would be classified with *this* and *that, some, one* and so on. With this classification one has the sneaking suspicion that it makes more sense than the conventional classification.

Using more than one open sentence in classification has the advantage that divisions between types of words which would otherwise be grouped together can be made. For instance, if a division between participles and adjectives is wanted, the open sentence

The boy was ———— *down the street*

allows *kicked* and *running* but not *fat* or *green*. Equally, of course, most participles have morphological signs of what they are, though this does not allow for irregular verbs (*see, saw*) nor words which look morphologically like participles but are not (*sling*, for instance which looks like the present participle of *sly*).

This much at least seems clear: that with a good deal of experimental work, it should be possible to make up a network of, say, twenty-five open sentences which effectively make every classification anyone could want. There are also other conditions which might be added to the notion of ALLOWABLE SUBSTITUEND to make classification better: for instance, we could specify that allowable substituends had to be such that substitution resulted in a sentence which could conceivably be true or false. This would remove problems over semi-poetic sentences, semantic nonsense and so on.

The objection to this way of classifying words is mainly practical.

The work of finding allowable substituends would all have to be done by educated native speakers of the language just because, on each trial, a judgement would have to be made as to whether the result of substitution was in fact a grammatically well formed sentence or not. In addition, though educated native speakers of a language have no difficulty, in the ordinary way, in distinguishing between well and ill formed sentences of the language, to do so self-consciously hour after hour is probably psychologically impossible. Add to this that there are at least some borderline cases in the matter of being a well formed sentence and the task is seen as a stark practical impossibility.

However, this impossibility does not mean the task must be abandoned. The reason that the open sentence

The _____ boy walked to the bus-stop

catches adjective-like words is that the variable has *the* in front of it and a noun after it. In general, when one finds a word in this sort of position in a sentence it will always be adjective-like (in fact, this could be the definition of a new classification). Furthermore, if more than one occurrence of the word is available (i.e., we are inspecting several sentences and the same word occurs in more than one of them), we will be able to classify it more precisely. For instance, we can note whether it also appears with the morphological variations associated with the comparative and superlative or with the morphological variations usual to a verb.

These ideas can be generalized. For the sort of verbal environment a word has in a grammatically well formed sentence we can, anyway sometimes, tell what part of speech it is. This technique, of course, depends on our knowing what the parts of speech are which surround the word which interests us. This problem is discussed below. In addition, knowing the sort of verbal environment a word has is usually insufficient to set its part of speech, partly because it may be more than one part of speech (anyway conventionally, but presumably in any new classification as well) and partly for the sorts of reasons discussed above. That is, a word which appears for A in

It was A,

salva grammaticale, may be four different parts of speech in conventional grammar and at least more than one, presumably, in any
future, rational grammar. However, this is not important: to find
out everything (either semantic of grammatical) about a word from
inspecting one occurrence of it is, in general, impossible (and undesirable; the point about language is that it is flexible). Equally, it
is not until many sentences are inspected that we can find out what
sort of morphological variations a word takes, and this can be an
important guide to classification. However, we now have an obvious way to try mechanical classification of parts of speech; that is,
by using the devices of noticing a word's verbal environment, what
morphological variations it takes and, of course, its relation to the
beginning and the end of the sentence.

If English (or any other natural language) were morphologically
entirely regular, noting what morphological variations words take
would be the ideal way to start a mechanical classification of parts
of speech. It would not produce every classification wanted (it
would, presumably, lump together all those words which take no
morphological variation) but it would give an important over-
classification which could be refined using the notion of verbal
environment. However, no natural language is entirely regular in
its morphological variation, not only in that, e.g., participles of
verbs are formed irregularly, but also because there are sets of
words of English which appear to be morphological variations of
one word when they are, in fact, different words. For instance, we
have the set *be, beer, best,* which does not make *be* an adjective,
nor *beer* a comparative. It is the second difficulty which makes this
approach unsuitable as the primary method of classification.[2]

Thus, though morphological variation can be taken as a hint for
classification, it is verbal environment which must be used as the
primary classification device. However, this seems to be a virtually
impossible method of proceeding, for it requires classification by
verbal environment where the words in the environment also lack
classification. The situation is not quite as bad as it appears to be

[2]   However, it can have a real practical use. This is discussed in the next chapter.

because the position of a word in relation to the two ends of the sentence can be known. However, this alone is insufficient. To classify the parts of speech mechanically, it is necessary to know at least some of the grammatical properties of at least some of the words of the language. How we can pick such words is the subject of the next chapter.

10

A JOIN BETWEEN SEMANTICS AND SYNTACTICS

It is a standard procedural rule in works on linguistics that semantics and syntactics can be treated as independent of each other. It is also standard to disclaim this rule as anything more than a useful working hypothesis which, for practical purposes, should be pushed as far as it will go. In practice, this means that the rule is never questioned. It is my opinion that rigid adherence to this procedural rule, though it was doubtless of value at one time in work on linguistics, is seriously hampering advance today.

In this chapter I shall make a broad over-classification of words into three categories. This distinction is both semantic and grammatical. A rough and ready (and semantic) way to describe the categorization is to say that it depends primarily on the division between those words which have an application to items of the world and those which do not. The distinction is made precise by the technique of finding allowable substituends for open sentences, which is, or anyway has previously been taken to be, a method of grammatical classification. There seems to be no doubt that this grammatico-semantic distinction is completely genuine: that is, that it classifies words into completely natural semantic and grammatical categories.

CATEGORY I: Those words, and their morphological variants, but excluding pronouns and numerals,[1] which have a conceivable

[1] Pronouns and numerals are special in many ways and need to be held to one side. This is not important because they form such a very small proportion of the language: in English there are about a hundred pronouns and numerals. That the number is so small is not surprising. There must be recursive rules for forming the number series and the number of discrete number words can therefore be kept very small. The only basis on which they could be increased is by

application to objects, events, situations, and so on, in the world. These words can be identified by noting that they are not pronouns or numerals and are substitutable into one or more of the following open sentences to make a sentence which is, or under certain physical circumstances[2] could be, true in a context where identification is appropriate.

That is X.
He (she, it) is X.

Examples: *That is water*; *He is sleeping*; *It is red.*

That (he, she, it) is a(n) X.

Examples: *That is a table*; *That is an elephant.*

That is an example of X.
That sort of thing (person) is X.

Example: *That is an example of fair-play*; *That sort of person is your neighbor* (remember the parable of the Good Samaritan).

If there were such a thing as (description) it would be correct to call it an X.

Examples: such words as *unicorn* and *satyre*. Then, where *I* is one of the words which fulfill the above conditions,

That (he, she, it) is a(n) X I.
That (he, she, it) is X I.

Examples: *That is real cream*; *He is an utter idiot*; *It is imitation caviar.* When *I* is one of the words which fulfill the above conditions,

That (he, she, it) is I X.

---

giving special names to very large numbers which now have no name (10^{30}, for instance, which, so far as I know, has no name) or by increasing the number base which we use (from 10 to 12, say). Similar considerations govern pronouns; their number could only be increased by adding more genders to the language or paying more attention to variant forms (*thee* for *you*). The general reason why both pronouns and numerals are special is that they are referential words with peculiarities about their method of reference and what they refer to.

[2] The phrase *physical circumstances* encompasses possible states of the world, not possible states of language, i.e., it does not include the possibility that language may have changed in certain ways.

Examples: *He is coming soon* (this type of open sentence is only necessary to accommodate adverbs which have no morphological form as adjectives).

CATEGORY II. Those words which have no such application (i.e., those words which are not pronouns or numerals and do not fit appropriately into the open sentences) even when morphologically varied, but which are necessary for connected utterances; most obviously such words as *and, in, of, the* (as I understand the term PARTICLE as grammarians use it, Category II includes all particles). Words in Category I have a meaning in an entirely straightforward way, we might say, while Category II words do not have a meaning in this straightforward way, though they do have a completely necessary function. Category II includes those words which Fries called FUNCTION WORDS, but some other words as well (auxiliary verbs, for instance).

CATEGORY III. Pronouns and numerals (both serial and cardinal).

It is interesting to make some purely empirical observations about the words in these three categories. The first category comprises (in the conventional classification) most (but not all) verbs, nouns, adjectives and adverbs, at least by morphological variation. Category I comprises, in fact, the vast majority of words in the language. For instance, a random count of 1078 words of a concise dictionary gives: Category I words: 1074; Category II words: 2; Category III words: 2.[3] As most esoteric and technical words are Category I words, using a concise dictionary biased the count in favor of Category II and Category III words. If one takes a full vocabulary of English (that is, including technical terms from chemistry, medicine, the law and so on) it contains upwards of 50,000 words; of this vocabulary, Category II and Category III words would comprise about one tenth of one percent. This, of course, does not give a measure of how important Category II and Category III words are in our use of the language. They are, as we all know, enormously

[3]   The actual count went as follows: the dictionary was opened at random at *rest* and we stopped at *semester*. We thus obtained: Nouns: 600; Verbs: 237; adjectives: 195; adverbs: 42; pronouns: 2; prepositions: 2; conjunctions: 0. A word which appeared both as a noun and a verb (there are many such words in English) was counted twice, once as a noun and once as a verb.

important. A random sampling of three prose passages showed that 27% of all words used were Category II words (there were, of course, many repetitions).

Because this classification into Category I words is achieved by the method of finding allowable substituends for open sentences it would appear that there will be no mechanical way to carry out this over-classification. This is not the case. That is, there are at least rough and ready ways in which, given a great many grammatically well formed sentences of English, this over-classification could be made mechanically, though this technique alone would not work perfectly for the highly inflected areas of language. The technique is this: Category I words have mechanically recognizable morphological variants where Category II words do not; Category III words have standard morphological variants which Category I words do not have (e.g. *seven* and *seventh*, *him* and *himself*). In general, of course, Category II and Category III words need cause no trouble just because a complete list of them is relatively easy to produce by hand.

With this distinction, I complete all the necessary theoretical work to write a language learning and analyzing program for the computer.

11

COMPUTERISING THE THEORY

At this point it is worth recalling where we are going and what has so far been accomplished.

For reasons explained in the Introduction, I was interested in writing a language learning and analysis program for the computer which would take grammatically well formed sentences of the English language as data and produce as output a 'dictionary' which would (a) list the words fed in as parts of the data sentences classified as to grammatical type and (b) go part of the way towards defining at least some of them in philosophically interesting ways. We will consider what progress has been made on these problems, taking the two parts of it in turn.

(a) Fries' technique for classifying words of the language, even when modified to remove the concept of STRUCTURAL MEANING, is impractical because it requires the self-conscious recognition of grammatically well formed sentences of the language for case after case. The answer to this problem is to reverse the procedure; that is, to start with grammatically well formed sentences. There is no difficulty about this; though there are borderline cases with the notion of a grammatically well formed sentence, there is no shortage of sentences which are undoubtedly grammatically well formed. Any one of these sentences may be regarded as an instantiation of a one-variable open sentence. By using this technique, we have a theoretically possible way to identify (newly defined) parts of speech by verbal environment in a grammatically well formed sentence. However, this technique alone is insufficiently sophisticated. At a conservative estimate, it would give us about 50 different parts of speech and one word would be a great many different parts of speech. The number itself is not very important but for any Chomskyesque generative grammar we must have more stable parts of speech than such a procedure would give. This difficulty is not very serious; it is not odd that the fact that a word appears in a certain position in ONE sentence (even if the grammatical type of every other word in the sentence is known) is insufficient to usefully set its grammatical type. However, using the data about a word which comes from noting its verbal environment in a GREAT MANY grammatically well formed sentences, it should be possible to cut the parts of speech down substantially and thus obtain more stable classifications. If, in addition, we use the types of morphological variation a word takes as at least clues to its classification, we should have a method of classification which is entirely stable.

There is a further difficulty: mechanical classification of words using these techniques cannot start until the grammatical type, or at least the grammatical functioning, of some words of the language is known. Thus, we must investigate which sorts of words must be understood in advance and how many such words; clearly if the number is too large the results will be uninteresting and if the group is too heterogeneous there will not be the faintest suggestion that it is logically sound, i.e., we will have found at best an empirical fact about an individual language, not some facet logically built into the notion of (anyway a certain type of) language. It is the empirical claim of this work that, if the functions of Category II and Category III words are understood, classification of every other word in the language is possible mechanically. This is only an empirical claim because I see no way of making it a logical claim. However, some logical claim of this type must be true. That is, granting that a language is learnable as a first language, it would seem that some such statement would be true about some class of words and the classification procedure used here does seem to be natural rather than artificial. However, these considerations hardly constitute a proof. In spite of this, 1 shall offer a further surmise: that all Category I words are mechanically classifiable on the basis of knowing the functions of non-Category I words for any language where the classification into Category I words and other words makes sense. I can see no way to substantiate this position, which is the reason I label it a surmise.

My principle thesis here, that if the functions of Category II and Category III words are understood then classification of every other word in the language is possible mechanically, receives some substantial confirmation, which is given in the next chapter. However, the nature of the substantiation must be understood. It is not claimed that all the conventional classifications can be obtained in this way (though most, in fact, could be). Indeed, granting that we now realize how arbitrary some conventional classifications are, it is undesirable that this is what should be produced. What is needed is a rigorous and precise classification. This is obtained. Furthermore, it does little violence to the conventional system in that, for instance, the central cases of the conventional noun become central cases of the newly defined substantive. In general, it is only borderline cases of present classification which suffer any sort of change.

Basing a classification on all of Category II and Category III words may seem to be using a rather large base set. In terms of sheer numbers, this is not the case: there appear to be under a thousand such words in English. In addition, there are ways, discussed in the next chapter, for cutting down this number substantially. That is, there are ways to mechanically classify Category I and Category II words on the basis of a small sub-set of these words.

(b) The second aim of the program was to obtain certain types of semantic information about the words classified. Because the aim has now been limited to classifying Category I words, it is only these words which concern us.

If a computer takes as data just grammatically well formed sentences of the language then there is very little semantic information to be obtained from them. The point of Chomsky's examples of peculiar sentences which are grammatically well formed is that they make very little semantic sense. However, the source of grammatically well formed sentences can make a difference: it would be desirable to exclude oddities like *Colourless green ideas sleep furiously*, i.e., it would be desirable to exclude things which are laboratory products only. As I suggested earlier, the obvious source for grammatically well formed sentences is the text (not the headlines) of newspapers. Any sentence which appears in a newspaper article, and is not written within quotation marks (to exclude the cute sayings of children and the like) will be grammatically well formed and will, more importantly, have a communicative function, i.e., in this respect will be unlike *Colourless green ideas sleep furiously*. From this sort of grammatically well formed sentence semantic information is obtainable.

As was pointed out in Chapter 5, semantic rules are of at least two types. The point here is this. That a start at least can be made on detecting semantic rules involving entailment relations where I can now see no way in which semantic rules involving engagement relations can be detected, except in very limited and at present speculative ways. It will be remembered that saying that every word in the language is definable amounts to saying that every word in the language is surrounded by entailment relations sufficient to define it.[1] However, every word in the language is not definable, so detecting all the entailment relations surrounding a word does not exhaust its semantic content. To put it another way, engagement rules are needed as well as entailment rules. Thus even if a computer can detect entailment rules it cannot, on that basis, detect all semantic information about the words processed in this way. However, it is still important to detect the entailment rules which do surround a word. Doing so goes a long way towards laying out what philosophers sometimes call the logic of a word.[2] Very roughly, the engagement rules give the application of a word (the element which can be taught ostensively) while entailment rules give the logic of a word. This explains why a computer with no

[1] Accurately, it is not a word which is surrounded by entailment rules but certain open sentences in which the word occurs. However, this need not delay us here.

[2] THE LOGIC OF A WORD is a philosophers' term of art which, so far as I know, no one has seriously attempted to define. However, what is said here is at least reasonably close to what philosophers have said about it. See Appendix III, Sections #7 and # .

counterpart to sensory apparatus can detect the latter and not the former.

The most obvious method of detecting entailment rules mechanically is this. Consider the word W which is bound by the following entailment rule:

X is W ENTAILS X is V,

where X is a variable but W is an actual word and V an actual word or phrase. If this rule holds, then it is pointful on occasions to say

The W is V,

or   Every W is V.

However, it is never pointful to use as the subject of a sentence the phrase

The V W ...

(It is not, in fact, pointful to use V W as a phrase anywhere in a sentence but let us keep it simple for the present.) To take an obvious example, it is pointful to say

A triangle is three cornered

or   *Every triangle is three cornered*

where it is never pointful to use as the subject of a sentence

The three cornered triangle ...

just because being a triangle entails having three corners. This is perhaps better seen where the entailment rule does not hold. The following rule does not hold.

X is a man ENTAILS X is breathing.

If it did hold, the phrase

The breathing man ...

would have no pointful use. But of course it does have a pointful use (the entailment relation does not hold). If, for some reason, every person in the room but one is known to be holding his breath, the phrase *The breathing man* has a perfectly good use. With this example, because the rule is nearly correct, we have to think of special circumstances in which the V W phrase has a use. But there is no pointful use for *The unmarried bachelor.*

There are, of course, several different open sentences which can be used in this technique for detecting entailment rules. However, the general point is now obvious. When a word can take simple[3] predication of another word or short phrase but cannot take that word or short phrase in a qualifying position, then there is an entailment rule between that word and what was originally predicated of it.

This technique will not detect every entailment rule surrounding a word. In particular, it will not detect entailment rules where V, in the schematic example, is a long phrase, just because long phrases never appear in a qualifying position. Nor will it detect entailment relations which have to be discovered in the sense in which the disciplines of philosophy and mathematics involve the discovery of entailment relations. This amounts to saying that this technique will only find trivial entailments. The last is an advantage: it is only trivial entailment rules which give the semantic content of a word. The first is a disadvantage and one which I do not at present see any way round.

In practice, detecting entailment rules in this way involves the following procedures. The computer takes as data grammatically well formed sentences which are pointful. It must then note, for every noun,[4] what adjectival qualification it takes on every one of its occurrences; and, for each adjective and adjectival phrase, when it appears in a simple predicative position, what noun in the subject it is predicated of. When sufficient information of this type has been accumulated (and SUFFICIENT will be a lot) the semantic rule will be obtainable entirely mechanically. However, more will be achieved than that. For a great many nouns and adjectives, there will be a mass of information on what sorts of predicates they can take or what they can be predicated of. Clearly this information is also important in logically (semantically) typing a word. Presumably there will be some way to detect at least some engagement rules.

---

[3] SIMPLE PREDICATION is predication using a part of the verb to be or to have, perhaps as auxiliaries.
[4] I have used the conventional classificatory words here. It will be seen later that this does not introduce inaccuracies.

Equally, some form of collation should be possible to form a type of thesaurus (which would be highly desirable). However, I am not now sure how this is to be done. Certainly the approach must be highly empirical. It is clear that if one had such information about a large number of words there are some highly interesting hypotheses which could be tried immediately and these, even if they failed, would lead to further hypotheses.

In what I have said so far about the mechanical detection of semantic information I have spoken only of nouns and adjectives. This is not as great a limitation as it appears to be. As we all know, most words of English have morphological variants which take them into the realm of nouns and adjectives. Those which do not will not yield to this technique of semantic analysis.

I have now outlined techniques by which, on the basis of being given all Category II and Category III words, a computer could, at least in principle, output a 'dictionary' which classifies all Category I words as to grammatical type and provides at least some semantic information about each. I also said that there were techniques by which we could avoid giving the computer all of the Category II and Category III words; these are discussed in the next Chapter.

There are several further techniques which have to be mentioned before the general claim made above can be illustrated in detail. The operation of classifying a Category I word as to grammatical type will often depend on having previously classified some other word in Category I. When this previous classification has not taken place, what is to be done? The answer is that nothing should be done. With any learning process or program, if the data is not chosen with a view to making learning proceed ideally, it will be found that at a certain stage in the learning process the learner gets data he (it) cannot handle. In that case, the data should just be ignored (perhaps noting that it has been, perhaps storing it for later processing). Secondly, the notion of an intelligent and correctable guess (i.e., self correction procedures) must be used. As we have seen, one occurrence of a word in a grammatically well formed sentence will not necessarily be enough to fix it as to grammatical type. This being so, it is necessary for the computer to make some tentative classifications which it will later correct or confirm in the light of subsequent data. Third, semantic information collected before a word is firmly classified as to grammatical type will itself be tentative and must be modifiable in the light of subsequent reclassification.

12

THE PILOT PROGRAM

In writing the pilot program I was constantly in difficulty because I was working with a very small computer.[1] As a result, there are many limitations on the pilot program which are in no way theoretically necessary.

The pilot program takes as data grammatically well formed sentences which are statemental in form and limited as to grammatical complexity. Its out-put is a 'dictionary' which lists the words fed in classified as to grammatical type and gives semantic information about them in ways outlined in the previous Chapter. The limitation on grammatical complexity was achieved by excluding sentences with internal punctuation and limiting sentence length. These limitations were entirely dictated by the size of the computer. In the most obvious instance, these limitations could have been lifted with a larger computer by having the computer take in sentences of any length but only processing sentences below a certain length. But this obvious way round is far cruder than necessary. It would have been simple to have the computer take in sentences of any length but frequently only process the first part of the sentence (subjects of sentences are in general easier to analyse than predicates). There is nothing odd about the program not processing certain data in the early stages of its running: children learning language clearly do this all the time. But because it is a learning program a sentence not processed early in the running of the program may well be processable later in the run. The actual

[1] The computer used was in fact an IBM 1620, Model II, with indirect addressing feature, 40,000 core-storage but no subsidiary memory.

pilot program notifies the operator when a sentence is not processed so that the sentence can be reoffered later in the run.

Both to save space and to make up for the drastic reduction in grammatical complexity involved in limiting sentence length, it seemed obvious to limit the number of Category II and Category III words whose grammatical function the computer commanded. In fact, the present program runs with the computer able to recognize initially only the following Category II words:

am	was	shall	not
are	were	may	never
is	have	can	
do	has	would	
does	had	could	
did	will	must	

These twenty Category II words represent about 2% of the totality of Category II and Category III words: the rest were classified by the computer. The only further information the computer had was grammatical information about English, including rules for morphological variation.

I now give an artificial example of the classifying aspect of the program. The example is artificial in this sense: the program is designed to run with a very large number of sentences so that the learning and self-correction features have an opportunity to operate effectively. To provide a manageable example, I deliberately wrote sentences for this run so that the computer would accept all of them for processing, make few mistakes and correct most of the mistakes it did make. The results of a non-artificial (but still far too short) run are given in Appendices I and II.

The example: the following story (including the title, which is a sentence) was fed into the computer as data.

THE FOX IS CAPTURED

Three cats were on the fence. The fence is brown. The largest cat was grey. The middle cat was black. The smallest cat was yellow.

The grey cat is very large. The yellow cat is very small. The cats will jump down soon. A brown fox jumps over the fence. The cats will not sit idly by. One of them will chase the fox. All three cats have jumped down. The grey cat has run away. He will not capture the fox. He will run a mile. The other cats are chasing the fox. Capturing a fox can be hard. Cats and fox are running fast. The yellow cat is the fastest. He has captured the fox. The yellow cat is victorious.

One aspect of the learning feature of the program can be seen immediately. The sentence *A brown fox jumps over the fence* has none of the verbal forms, listed on the previous page, which the computer commands initially. As a consequence, had that sentence been offered to the computer as the first data-sentence it would have gone unprocessed because the computer would have had no way to start analysing it. In the actual run, the computer had already learned that *jump* is a verb and processed the sentence using that information.

The computer classified the words in the above story into the following grammatical categories:

S   = substantives
Q   = generically a qualifying word (not necessarily an adjective)
VQ = adverb
DQ = present participle of a verb
PQ = past participle of a verb
V   = verb
R   = relational word; roughly, a conjunction.
B   = a word which is no other part of speech and can begin a noun phrase.

(Pronouns come out in this classification as substantives — which, of course, they are.) Opposite certain entry numbers in the dictionary the word has been eliminated and it is noted that it was a morphological variant of some other word in the dictionary and therefore not worth individual listing.

DICTIONARY

Entry No.	Word	Class
001	FOX	S
002	THE	B
003	CAPTURED	PQ
004	MORPHOLOGICAL VARIANT OF 009	
005	THREE	Q
006	FENCE	S
007	ON	Q
008	BROWN	Q
009	CAT	S
010	MORPHOLOGICAL VARIANT OF 016	
011	GREY	Q
012	MIDDLE	Q
013	BLACK	Q
014	MORPHOLOGICAL VARIANT OF 018	
015	YELLOW	Q
016	LARGE	Q
017	VERY	Q
018	SMALL	Q
019	JUMP	V
020	SOON	Q
021	DOWN	Q
022	A	B
023	OVER	Q
024	SIT	V
025	BY	Q
026	IDLY	Q
027	THEM	S
028	OF	Q
029	ONE	B
030	CHASE	V
031	ALL	B
032	JUMPED	PQ
033	AWAY	Q
034	RUN	V
035	HE	S
036	CAPTURE	V
037	MILE	S
038	OTHER	Q
039	CHASING	DQ
040	CAPTURING	DQ

```
041           BE  V
042         HARD  Q
043          AND  R
044         FAST  Q
045      RUNNING  DQ
046 MORPHOLOGICAL VARIANT OF 044
047  VICTORIOUS Q
```

The word eliminated at 004 was *cats*, at 010 was *largest*, at 014 was *smallest*, and at 046 was *fastest*.

The dictionary contains mistakes: most obviously *by*, *on* and *of* should have been listed as R rather than Q words (*and* at 043 was correctly listed as R). This would have occurred on a longer run (see entries 007, 025, 028 in Appendix II). The other 'mistake' is that finer distinctions among the Qs are made on a longer run and a further classification (VS), for words which are both substantives and verbs, is employed.

When the program runs, processing sentences is accomplished by starting at the verb and working first towards the beginning of the sentence and then towards the end. In the initial instance (i.e., when no dictionary entries have yet been made) it works primarily by position in the sentence (in relation both to the position of the verb and the end of the sentence) but to some extent by taking clues from suffixes. All classifications which take place at this stage must be looked upon (and are looked upon by the computer) as guesses which have to be modified or confirmed later: it is when such modification or confirmation has not taken place that mistakes of classification usually occur. The computer then reads the next sentence and the same process is followed. However, as the program runs the computer confirms or modifies classifications on words already listed and utilizes previous classifications to analyse the sentence currently being processed. There are many ways this can be done. If, for instance, one has this formation (where X is the word to be classified)

$$S + X + S$$

X is classifiable as R. Equally for

$$S + X + B +.$$

X must be V or R. This, of course, does not only work for R words. If one has

$$The + X + R +$$
or $$B + X + R +$$

X is classifiable as S. Clearly these techniques do not require limitation on sentence length or grammatical complexity and it is by using such techniques that the program can be seen to be extendable to cover sentences of any length or complexity.

These are the ways sentences can be analysed as they enter the computer. As the dictionary grows, past analyses are utilized. However, it is often the case that a later classification should alter or modify an earlier one. It is therefore necessary to pause in processing data fairly frequently to compare items already in the dictionary. This process, called in this program the SHAKE operation, takes place automatically every ten sentences. Primarily the SHAKE operation looks for morphological variation. However, it is not just a matter of looking for the usual suffixes because finding such a suffix does not guarantee that the word is of some one definite grammatical type. For instance, *silly* is not an adverb, *need* is not the past participle of either *ne* or *nee*, etc. (it is for this reason that the usual examples given to show how well English is structured, for instance examples like *A woggle ugged a diggle*,[2] are so very deceptive). Thus, if a word with one of the usual suffixes is found, the rest of the dictionary must be searched for that word without the suffix. If such a word is found, and if it is already classified in an appropriate way (which often means not in some one definite way), then there is a basis for fairly certain classification. If a reclassification of a relevant word takes place, it will be taken account of in the next SHAKE operation. The condition that a word found as a possible morphological variant of another word should already be classified in an appropriate way is most important. Without it, *best* would be considered to be the superlative form of *be*, *thing* the present participle of *the*, *her* the comparative of *he* and

---

[2] From Fries, *The Structure of English*, where just the point here criticised is made.

so on. There is another routine, called DESTRUCTIVE SHAKE, intro-
duced by switches at the end of the processing of a set of sentences.
This routine is identical to SHAKE except that it eliminates unnecessary morphological variants of words already in the dictionary,
noting that it is doing so, and does one or two other minor clean-up
operations before reading-out the dictionary.

The program is designed to run with a large number of sentences
where the same word is used many times and morphologically
varied. If this condition is fulfilled, mistakes in classification (granting that the classification is not conventional) are very rare. They
occur primarily when (a) a word has, in fact, only appeared once
in the data sentences and the original unconfirmed guess is allowed
to stand and (b) in the very highly inflected areas of English. That
is, the computer will recognize that *eyes* is the plural of *eye* but it
will never realize that *men* is the plural of *man*. Any program designed to learn English completely will inevitably have to have
some correcting procedure such that it can be told (as a child is
told) that, irrational though it may be, *children* not *childs* is the
plural of *child*.

Recording the sort of semantic information outlined in the last
chapter was theoretically fairly easy. In addition, I knew that I was
not going to be able to store enough semantic information to get
the computer to work on that information usefully. However, I
decided to record such information as I could to make sure that the
serial operation of first classifying (and perhaps re-classifying) a
word grammatically and then locating its semantic connections was
as straightforward as it seemed to be. The following two procedures
were employed: (a) If a substantive was qualified by some word, the
computer listed the entry number for the substantive with the entry
for the qualifying word. Thus the following would be a typical
dictionary entry for a qualifying word:

Entry No.	Word	Class	Semantic connections
072	BLACK	Q	003,071,053,231,153

The numbers under SEMANTIC CONNECTIONS give the entry numbers of the substantives which may take *black* as qualification. The above entry might indicate that cats, rugs, chessmen, pipes and tires can be black. (b) If a substantive appeared in the subject of a sentence and the predicate contained a simple qualifying word, then the entry number of the qualifying word was entered after the substantive. If the verb was negated, this was indicated by placing a bar over the left hand end of the entry number. Thus, with such sentences as *Cats are animals*, the entry for *animal* would contain, under SEMANTIC CONNECTIONS, the entry number for *cat*; if the sentence had been *Cats are not animals* the entry number would have had a bar placed over its left hand digit. I now realize that this procedure was too simple: it should have been followed only when the verb in the data sentence is part of *to be* or *to have*. In all other instances, it is the entry number of the verb which should have gone under SEMANTIC CONNECTIONS in the listing for the substantive. Ideally, of course, whole predicates should have been stored but that would have required much larger storage than was available.

Implemented in the ways indicated, the program runs entirely satisfactorily. Appendices I and II give the details of as long a run as the small computer available could handle — it is, in fact, far too short a run. Appendix II gives the dictionary produced from these sentences. It will be seen that the dictionary contains misclassifications, though very few. These errors could have been eliminated by the addition of some judiciously chosen sentences, designed precisely for this purpose; but for obvious reasons this has not been done. However, there is little doubt that with a longer run these misclassifications could be eliminated: it is notable that they mostly occur at the end of the dictionary rather than at the beginning. This occurs, of course, because entries near the end are usually for words which appeared only once in the data sentences.

13

APPENDIX I: SENTENCES

```
THE FOX IS CAPTURED
THREE CATS WERE ON THE FENCE
THE FENCE IS BROWN
THE LARGEST CAT WAS GREY
THE MIDDLE CAT WAS BLACK
THE SMALLEST CAT WAS YELLOW
THE GREY CAT IS VERY LARGE
THE YELLOW CAT IS VERY SMALL
THE CATS WILL JUMP DOWN SOON
A BROWN FOX JUMPS OVER THE FENCE
THE CATS WILL NOT SIT IDLY BY
ONE OF THEM WILL CHASE THE FOX
ALL THREE CATS HAVE JUMPED DOWN
THE GREY CAT HAS RUN AWAY
HE WILL NOT CAPTURE THE FOX
HE WILL RUN A MILE
THE OTHER CATS ARE CHASING THE FOX
CAPTURING A FOX CAN BE HARD
CATS AND FOX ARE RUNNING FAST
THE BLACK CAT HAS A BROWN BROTHER
THE TALL GIRL WILL NOT SING
NOW THE DOG IS CHASING THE CAT
AN ANIMAL IS NOT ALWAYS FURRY
A CAT IS AN ANIMAL
THEREFORE A CAT IS NOT ALWAYS FURRY
CATS DO NOT CHASE DOGS
THE BOY WAS NOT IN THE HOUSE
NO CAT IS GREEN
THE BOY WILL KICK THE CAT
HE IS A NASTY BOY
SOME CATS HAVE VERY LONG TAILS
DOGS DO NOT RUN FAST
```

THAT BOY IS EASILY STRONGER
SOME BIG BOYS ARE STRONG
THE GIRL IS WEALTHIER
HE IS UNDOUBTEDLY WEALTHY
SOME CATS ARE BLACK
THE CAT IS BLACK
A LARGE CAT HAS A LONG TAIL
THE SCISSORS ARE FOR CUTTING THINGS
TAILS ARE FURRY
BOYS AND GIRLS ARE PLAYING AND DANCING
THE USUAL BOY WAS HERE TODAY
BUT LARGER BOYS ARE USUALLY STRONGER
MEN LIKE ION ARE EASY TO LIKE
LOVE HAS MANY FACES
THE GIRL WILL GO TO HEAVEN
BLACK CATS HAVE GREEN EYES
ALL DOGS HAVE TAILS
ALL DOGS CHASE CATS
ALL THE CATS JUMP OVER THE DOG
ALL THE GIRLS HAVE LONG HAIR
ALL THE MEN WERE LONELY
ALL BLACK CATS ARE EVIL
THE BOY WILL GO HOME
THE BOY HAS SOME MATCHES
NOW HE HAS STRUCK A MATCH
ANY LARGE BOY IS STRONG
THE BLACK CAT HAS A LONG TAIL
THE BOY STUPIDLY KICKED THE DOG
THE BOY KICKED THE BALL
THE OTHER BOY IS THE STRONGEST
ONE EYE IS BETTER THAN FIVE
PATIENCE IS A VIRTUE
THE DOG HAS A TAIL
THE BOY WAS ALWAYS A LONE WOLF
THE BOY WILL KICK THE BALL
THE BOY WAS ON THE FLOOR
SANDY WILL CHASE THE DOGS
THE BOYS CHASE THE DOGS
ONE EYE IS BETTER THAN NONE
THE BLACK CAT HAS GREEN EYES
THE CAT HAS A TAIL
THE DOG IS BY THE CAT
BOYS AND GIRLS ARE GOOD FRIENDS

THE BOY HAS NO TAIL
MANY BOYS ARE DIRTY
SOME GIRLS ARE DIRTY MINDED
A BOY HAS TWO LEGS
THE DOG IS CHASING THE CAT
THE MAN IS ON THE FLOOR
THE CAT IS ON THE MAT
THE MAN IS BY THE CAT
A BOY IS A MALE ANIMAL
CATS ARE ANIMALS
THE CAT IS ON THE MAT
CATS OR DOGS ARE THE BEST PETS
JON HAS A BLACK CAT
THE BOY WAS STROKING THE CAT
THE GIRL WILL GO TO HEAVEN
THE CAT HAS LOST ITS TAIL
THE LARGE CAT WILL BE AWAY
THE BOYS WILL NOT DANCE OR SING
A CAT USUALLY HAS A LONG TAIL
THE USUAL DOG IS NOT HERE TODAY
THE DOG HAS LONG HAIR
THE BROWN CAT HAS A LARGE FACE
A DOG IS A GOOD FRIEND
THE CAT WAS BY THE DOOR
THE CAT WILL JUMP OVER THE DOG
THE BOY WILL NEVER COME TODAY
THE FOX WILL NOT EASILY COME
THE BOY DOES NOT RUN WELL
CATS RUN VERY FAST
CATS DO NOT LOVE QUIETLY
THE CAT DID NOT HAVE WHISKERS
THE CATS COME QUICKLY
THE GIRL WILL KICK THE DOG
THE BOY NEVER HAS HIS BOOKS
THE CATS DO NOT LIKE PLAYING
THE DOGS WILL NOT RUN AWAY
THE BROWN FOX RUNS OVER THE DOG
THE BOY WILL NOT WILLINGLY COME NOW
THE BOY IS THE WEALTHIEST
HERE IS A CAT
HIS NAME IS SANDY
SANDY IS VERY INTELLIGENT
SANDY HAS MANY WHISKERS

THE DOGS ARE TEASING SANDY
SANDY HAS ARCHED HIS BACK
SANDY IS SPITTING
THE BAD DOGS ARE DEFEATED
THEY ARE RUNNING AWAY
THE GREY WOLF WAS HUNGRY
BOYS OF STONE DO NOT LOVE
BOYS ON HORSES ARE DANGEROUS
THE LONGEST DIMENSION WAS THREE YARDS
A YARD IS THIRTY-SIX INCHES
AN INCH IS QUITE SMALL
THE FOOLISH BOY WAS ON THE FLOOR
MANY GIRLS SAY SILLY THINGS
THAT GIRL IS ALMOST SUBHUMAN
THE FOX IS ON THE TOWN
ALL THE FOXES CAN RUN
THE FOOLISH GIRL LOVED CANDY
CANDY IS VERY SWEET
THE STONE FLOOR WAS VERY HARD
THE STONE WAS ON THE FLOOR
THE UNDOUBTED GIRL WAS IN TROUSERS
THE GRASS IS GREEN
THE FAST CAR WAS BROWN
HER HAIR WAS VERY LONG
A BROTHER IS A MALE SIBLING
THE DOOR WAS GREEN
THE HOUSE HAD A GREEN DOOR
THE BOOK WAS ON THE GREY FLOOR
THE GIRL HAS NEVER HAD A DOG
THE BOY WILL HAVE GONE TO BED
THE TWO BOYS WILL NOT FIGHT
THE MAT IS ON THE FLOOR
IT WILL BE CLEANED QUICKLY
THE GIRL WILL CLEAN THE MAT
CLEANING THE MAT WILL BE EASY
THE MAT IS GAILY COLOURED
THE BOY IS GAY
THE MAT IS RED AND BLUE
THE MAT IS NOT BLACK
THE BOY MAY KICK THE DOG
BOYS KICK VERY HARD
THE GIRL MAY NOT GO TO HEAVEN
SOME BOYS TEASE CATS

```
ALL THE GIRLS WILL LOVE A MAN
THE GIRLS WILL TEASE THE GIRLS
A BLACK FLAG IS NOT LOVELY
THE MALE CAT WILL NOT SPIT
WE WILL BE COMING SOON
THE BLACK DOG WILL BE COMING SOON
THE BLACK DOG HAS LONG HAIR
SANDY WILL DEFEAT THE DOGS
HE WILL THINK OF SOMETHING
ALL GIRLS LOVE GEEGAWS
A GEEGAW IS A BRIGHT OBJECT
ALMOST ANYTHING IS AN OBJECT
MOST OBJECTS HAVE DIMENSIONS
MATERIAL OBJECTS HAVE THREE DIMENSIONS
THE BLACK DOG JUMPED OVER THE FOX
FOXES HAVE LONG TAILS
CATS AND DOGS NEVER LOVE EACH OTHER
THE BOY IS WILLING TO GO
SANDY HAS ONLY ONE WHISKER
DOGS AND CATS FIGHT EACH OTHER
THE TITLE IS GIVEN NEXT
THIS IS A STORY
FOX AND CATS ARE RUNNING FAST
SANDY MAY LIKE HIS DINNER
HIS PLACE IS BY THE WINDOW
THE LOW BED WAS IN THE CORNER
THE LARGE TOWN WAS BADLY LIT
THE GREY TROUSERS WERE ON THE FLOOR
THE CATS DEFEATED THE DOGS
THE BOYS TEASED THE DOGS
THE SMALL BOYS CLEANED THE HOUSE
DOGS AND CATS FIGHT ALL THE TIME
THE BROWN HORSE HAD A LONG TAIL
THE CAT WILL ARCH ITS BACK
THE GREY HORSE IS FRISKY
SOME GIRLS ARE FRISKY
SANDY ARCHED HIS BACK
FRISKY GIRLS USUALLY DANCE WELL
THE CLEAN GIRL WILL STROKE THE CAT
SANDY IS HIS PET
HIS HOME IS IN THE TOWN
ONE BRANCH WAS VERY THICK
HEAVEN AND HELL ARE MYTHICAL PLACES
```

THE BOYS LIKE THEIR DINNERS
THE LONG HOUSE IS NOT PAINTED BROWN
THE STUPID BOY WILL PAINT THE HOUSE
THE TALL BOY WOULD PAINT IT BETTER
THE BROWN CAT SINGS BY NIGHT
THE NIGHT IS ALWAYS BLACK
GIRLS ARE JUST ANIMALS
THE USUAL BOY WILL NOT COME TODAY
THE GREY WOLF IS AT THE DOOR
THE BROWN HOUSE HAS A DOOR
THE UNDOUBTED WOLF JUMPED OVER THE BOY
THE BOY WILL STROKE SANDY
THE BOY WAS HAPPY AFTER DINNER
THE ANIMALS WERE HAVING A FIGHT
SANDY WAS FIGHTING HARD
THE CATS WERE FIGHTING THE DOGS
THE CATS WILL UNDOUBTEDLY WIN
THE LARGE DOOR WAS PAINTED BLACK
THE SMALL DOOR WAS PAINTED YELLOW
THE NEXT STORY WILL BE ABOUT CARS
THE NEXT BOY WILL RUN QUICKLY
THE LONG STORY WILL BE ABOUT DOGS
THE BOY WAS BY THE GIRL
THE HARD STONE WAS USED FOR BUILDING
THE LARGE STONE WAS USED FOR THROWING
THE PAINTED STONE WAS ON THE FLOOR
THE MAN WILL BUILD A HOUSE
THE BOY WILL LIVE IN THE HOUSE
THE WEALTHY BOY WILL SPEND FREELY
THE BOY WILL MIND THE CAT
BOYS SPEND MONEY FAST
THE FOOLISH CAT HAD A SHORT TAIL
THE YELLOW CAT HAD A LONG TAIL
THE LARGE DOOR WAS LOCKED
THE SMALL DOOR WAS STUCK
THE BOY WILL NEVER LOCK THE DOOR
HE IS NOT STRONG ENOUGH
THE BOYS WILL PLAY TODAY
THEY PLAY WELL
THE TALL TREE HAD MANY BRANCHES
THE SHORT TREE HAD SHORT BRANCHES
A GOOD DINNER IS A LOVESOME THING
SANDY LIKES TO PLAY

```
HE WILL PLAY WITH ION
A GAY GIRL CAN CUT MUSTARD
MUSTARD IS A TART VEGETABLE
A GEEGAW IS A THING
THE BOY IS IN A TEMPER
THE BOY IS IN A BOAT
THE HOUSE IS VERY LARGE INDEED
THE SMALL GIRLS SING WELL
THE LARGE GIRLS SIT BY THE FIRE
SANDY WILL NEVER SAY ANYTHING
GAY GIRLS GO VESTLESS
BOYS ON HORSES ARE DANGEROUS
THE HOUSE IS VERY SMALL
GIRLS LOVE MONEY
BOYS LOVE GIRLS
THAT IS AN ENIGMA
THE YELLOW CAT IS THE LARGEST
HE HAS CAPTURED THE FOX
THE YELLOW CAT IS VICTORIOUS
BOYS BY THEMSELVES ARE OFTEN SILLY
GIRLS IN CARS ARE FREQUENTLY SILLY
ONE LEG IS BETTER THAN NONE
HIS BACK IS VERY STRAIGHT
HIS TROUSERS ARE WELL PRESSED
SOMETHING IS ALWAYS THE MATTER
THE WINDOW IS OPEN
THE BOY IS IN THE CORNER
BOYS AT PLAY ARE NOISY
THE MONEY WAS ON THE FLOOR
THE PLAY WAS EXCELLENT
THE DANCE WAS VERY FULL
ONE TROUSER IS NOT POSSIBLE
THE BOAT WAS BEAUTIFUL
I WOULD CHOOSE CATS OVER DOGS
```

The following four sentences were rejected when first offered to the computer. They were reoffered at the end of the run and were then accepted.

```
MANY GIRLS SAY SILLY THINGS
THE FOOLISH GIRL LOVED CANDY
SOME BOYS TEASE CATS
SANDY ARCHED HIS BACK
```

14

APPENDIX II: DICTIONARY

```
NO      WORD     CLASS   SEMANTIC CONNECTIONS
001        FOX   S 027,035,009,050,035,
002        THE   B
003     CAPTURED PQ
004 MORPHOLOGICAL VARIANT OF 009,
005      THREE   Q  004,009,
006      FENCE   S  001,
007         ON   R
008      BROWN   Q  001,009,235,058,
009        CAT   S  050,057,129,088,084,047,099,
                    121,
010 MORPHOLOGICAL VARIANT OF 016,
011       GREY   Q 009,117,119,
012     MIDDLE   Q  009,
013      BLACK   Q  009,
014 MORPHOLOGICAL VARIANT OF 018,
015     YELLOW   Q  009,
016      LARGE   Q 009,057,
017       VERY   Q
018      SMALL   Q 009,
019       JUMP   V
020       SOON   Q
021       DOWN   Q
022          A   B
023       OVER   Q 099,
024        SIT   V
025         BY   R
026       IDLY   Q
027       THEM   S
028         OF   R
029        ONE   B
```

```
030        CHASE  V
031          ALL  B
032       JUMPED  PQ
033         AWAY  Q
034          RUN  V
035           HE  S
036      CAPTURE  V
037         MILE  S  035,
038        OTHER  Q  009,057,
039       CHASING  DQ
040     CAPTURING  DQ
041           BE  V
042         HARD  Q  161,
043          AND  R
044         FAST  Q  182,009,
045      RUNNING  DQ
046       BROTHER  S  009,
047         GIRL  S  198,057,121,
048         TALL  Q  047,057,270,
049         SING  V
050          DOG  S  009,004,057,120,121,009,047,
                      001,225,307,
051          NOW  B
052       ANIMAL  S  009,057,047,
053           AN  B
054        FURRY  Q
055       ALWAYS  Q
056    THEREFORE  B
057          BOY  S  035,117,
058        HOUSE  S  121,057,129,
059           IN  R
060           NO  B
061        GREEN  Q
062         KICK  V
063        NASTY  Q
064         SOME  B
065 MORPHOLOGICAL VARIANT OF 075,
066         LONG  Q  100,164,
067         THAT  S
068 MORPHOLOGICAL VARIANT OF 071,
069       EASILY  VQ
070          BIG  Q  057,
071       STRONG  Q  057,
```

```
072 MORPHOLOGICAL VARIANT OF 073,
073      WEALTHY   Q 057,
074 UNDOUBTEDLY VQ
075          TAIL   S 009,050,057,235,
076    SCISSORS   S
077 MORPHOLOGICAL VARIANT OF 275,
078      CUTTING DQ
079          FOR Q
080      DANCING DQ
081      PLAYING DQ
082        USUAL Q  057,050,
083        TODAY Q
084         HERE   S
085 MORPHOLOGICAL VARIANT OF 016,
086          BUT B
087      USUALLY VQ
088          ION   S 035,
089         LIKE   V
090          MEN   S
091           TO Q
092         EASY Q
093         LOVE VS 009,161,
094 MORPHOLOGICAL VARIANT OF 139,
095         MANY Q  057,198,
096           GO   V
097       HEAVEN   S
098 MORPHOLOGICAL VARIANT OF 111,
099 MORPHOLOGICAL VARIANT OF 050,
100         HAIR   S 050,
101       LONELY VQ
102         EVIL Q
103         HOME   S
104 MORPHOLOGICAL VARIANT OF 105,
105        MATCH   S 057,
106       STRUCK Q
107          ANY   B
108     STUPIDLY VQ
109         BALL   S 057,
110 MORPHOLOGICAL VARIANT OF 071,
111          EYE   S
112         FIVE Q
113         THAN Q
114       BETTER Q
```

```
115     PATIENCE   S
116       VIRTUE   S 115,
117         WOLF   S
118         LONE   Q
119        FLOOR   S 161,185,130,233,263,
120        SANDY   S 151,050,057,
121 MORPHOLOGICAL VARIANT OF 057,
122         NONE   Q
123 MORPHOLOGICAL VARIANT OF 140,
124         GOOD   Q   226,
125        DIRTY   Q
126       MINDED   PQ
127 MORPHOLOGICAL VARIANT OF 294,
128          TWO   Q   121,
129          MAN   S 198,
130          MAT   S 047,
131         MALE   Q 009,
132           OR   R
133         BEST   Q
134 MORPHOLOGICAL VARIANT OF 239,
135     STROKING   DQ
136 MORPHOLOGICAL VARIANT OF 189,
137         LOST   Q
138        DANCE   V
139         FACE   S 009,
140       FRIEND   S 050,
141         DOOR   S 058,117,057,
142         COME   V
143         WELL   Q
144      QUIETLY   Q
145 MORPHOLOGICAL VARIANT OF 218,
146      QUICKLY   Q
147 MORPHOLOGICAL VARIANT OF 185,
148          HIS   Q 297,154,
149    WILLINGLY   VQ
150 MORPHOLOGICAL VARIANT OF 073,
151         NAME   S
152  INTELLIGENT   Q
153      TEASING   DQ 120,
154         BACK   S 120,
155       ARCHED   PQ
156     SPITTING   DQ
157          BAD   Q   050,
```

```
158    DEFEATED PQ
159       THEY   S
160     HUNGRY Q
161      STONE  S
162 MORPHOLOGICAL VARIANT OF 235,
163   DANGEROUS Q
164   DIMENSION  S 211,
165 MORPHOLOGICAL VARIANT OF 066,
166 MORPHOLOGICAL VARIANT OF 167,
167       YARD  S
168 MORPHOLOGICAL VARIANT OF 170,
169  THIRTY-SIX Q
170      INCH   S
171     QUITE  Q
172    FOOLISH Q   057,009,047
173   SUBHUMAN Q
174    ALMOST  Q
175      TOWN   S 103,
176 MORPHOLOGICAL VARIANT OF 001,
177     CANDY  S 047,
178     SWEET  Q
179   UNDOUBTED Q   047,117,
180 MORPHOLOGICAL VARIANT OF 304,
181     GRASS  S
182       CAR  S 225,
183       HER  B
184    SIBLING  S 046,
185      BOOK  S
186       BED  S
187      GONE  Q
188     FIGHT  V
189        IT  S 057,075,
190    CLEANED PQ
191     CLEAN  V
192    CLEANING DQ
193    COLOURED Q
194     GAILY  VQ
195       GAY  Q   047,198,
196      BLUE  Q
197       RED  Q
198 MORPHOLOGICAL VARIANT OF 047,
199     TEASE  V
200      FLAG   S
```

```
201        LOVELY VQ
202          SPIT  V
203            WE  S
204        COMING DQ
205        DEFEAT  V
206         THINK  V
207     SOMETHING  S
208 MORPHOLOGICAL VARIANT OF 209,
209        GEEGAW  S
210        BRIGHT Q
211        OBJECT  S 209,212,
212      ANYTHING  S 120,
213          MOST Q  211,
214      MATERIAL Q  211,
215 MORPHOLOGICAL VARIANT OF 001,
216          EACH Q
217       WILLING Q
218       WHISKER  S
219          ONLY VQ
220           HOW  B
221         TITLE  S
222          NEXT Q  225,057,
223         GIVEN Q
224          THIS  S
225         STORY  S 224,
226        DINNER  S 121,057,
227         PLACE  S 240,
228        WINDOW  S
229           LOW Q  186,
230        CORNER Q
231           LIT Q
232         BADLY VQ
233 MORPHOLOGICAL VARIANT OF 304,
234          TIME  S 004,
235         HORSE  S
236          ARCH  V
237        FRISKY Q  198,
238        STROKE  V
239           PET  S 050
240          HELL  S
241      MYTHICAL Q
242         THEIR Q
243       PAINTED PQ
```

```
244        STUPID Q  057,
245         PAINT  V
246         NIGHT  S
247          JUST Q
248            AT  R
249         AFTER  Q  226,
250         HAPPY Q
251         HAVING Q
252     FIGHTING DQ
253           WIN  V
254         ABOUT  Q 099,
255     BUILDING DQ
256          USED Q
257     THROWING Q
258         BUILD  V
259          LIVE  V
260         SPEND  V
261        FREELY Q
262          MIND  V
263         MONEY  S
264         SHORT  Q  270,
265        LOCKED PQ
266         STUCK Q
267          LOCK  V
268        ENOUGH Q
269          PLAY  V
270          TREE  S
271 MORPHOLOGICAL VARIANT OF 272,
272        BRANCH  S
273         THICK Q
274      LOVESOME Q
275         THING  S 226,209,
276          WITH Q  088,
277           CUT  V
278       MUSTARD  S
279          TART Q
280     VEGETABLE  S 278,
281        TEMPER Q
282          BOAT  S
283        INDEED Q
284          FIRE Q
285           SAY  V
286      VESTLESS Q
```

```
287        ENIGMA  S 067,
288 MORPHOLOGICAL VARIANT OF 044,
289   VICTORIOUS Q
290   THEMSELVES  S
291        SILLY Q
292        OFTEN Q
293   FREQUENTLY Q
294          LEG  S
295         THEN Q
296     STRAIGHT Q
297 MORPHOLOGICAL VARIANT OF 304,
298      PRESSED Q
299       MATTER Q
300         OPEN Q
301        NOISY Q
302    EXCELLENT Q
303         FULL Q
304      TROUSER  S
305     POSSIBLE Q
306    BEAUTIFUL Q
307            I  S
308       CHOOSE  V
```

15

APPENDIX III: FURTHER THEORIES OF MEANING

There are today three sophisticated theories about the meanings of words all of which have powerful adherents. The first theory is so unspecific that it is impossible to discuss it as a theory. Its popular statement is encompassed in the saying, "The meaning of a word is its use". In this form the theory is so inexplicit as to be no more than a rallying cry (what does *use* mean here?), though it is worth noticing that even in this form it does get a good deal of support. The historical origin of the theory is the occasion when Ludwig Wittgenstein, before the Moral Science Club at Cambridge in 1931, said about words: "Don't ask for the meaning, ask for the use." This, of course, does not constitute a theory of meaning but a piece of advice. His later statement of the theory is this: "For a LARGE class of cases — though not for all — in which we employ the word 'meaning' it can be defined thus: the meaning of a word is its use in the language" (*Philosophical Investigations*, section 40). But the ambiguity on USE is never resolved, nor is any explanation offered for the matter of "for a LARGE class of cases — though not for all —". I shall not discuss this theory itself because it is just too inexplicit to discuss. However, one of the theories which is discussed (the "Illocutionary Theory") is avowedly an attempt to rationalize and specify Wittgenstein's position. Equally, I do say a great deal about the notion of THE USE OF A WORD. If what is said about USE is correct, no obvious interpretation of Wittgenstein's theory can be correct.

The two theories which will be discussed are as follows:

THE CATEGORY DIFFERENCE THEORY. This theory, whose modern

exponent is Professor Gilbert Ryle,[1] consists in the following position: that there is a category difference between LANGUAGE and SPEECH. LANGUAGE is considered to be the body of words in any language and the grammatical and semantic rules for their correct employment; thus, LANGUAGE is what we learn when we learn a living language, like French or German. SPEECH, on the other hand, is an activity, namely chat or discourse, i.e., giving vent to utterances.[2] We indulge in this activity wherever we say anything in the normal sort of way. As an historical note, Ryle attributes this distinction to Alan Gardiner though I think its originator was the French linguist de Saussure.

THE ILLOCUTIONARY THEORY. The illocution of a given utterance is what it does, as opposed to what its effects are, in virtue of being the utterance it is. Thus the illocution of the utterance *I promise to do X* (instantiated) is PROMISING and of *The cat is on the mat*, on some occasion of its utterance, is probably STATING. The Illocutionary Theory is less well defined than the Category Difference Theory except in the work of Professor William Alston.[3] For the purposes of the present discussion, I offer the following statement of the position: The way to detect what an utterance means is to see what its illocution is, and words get their meaning derivatively from their use in utterances. More explicitly two utterances mean the same when they perform the same illocutionary act and two sentences mean the same when they have the same illocutionary act potential. This theory is represented by Alston as being a theory which makes the Wittgensteinian 'theory', presented above, true.

#2   At first glance, these two theories appear to be completely compatible, the second being a theory about the notion of LAN-

---

[1] Explicitly in "Use, Usage' and Meaning", *Proceedings of the Aristotelian Society* (Supplementary Volume), (1961). I also draw a good deal on his paper "Ordinary Language", *Philosophical Review* (1953).

[2] An UTTERANCE, as used here, is a datable event, i.e., the utterance of a sentence on some definite occasion, by a definite speaker, under definite circumstances, and so on (what Austin meant by a SPEECH ACT).

[3] In *The Philosophy of Language* (Englewood Cliffs, 1964). Also in "Meaning and Use", *Philosophical Quarterly* (1963).

GUAGE in the first. However, in the hands of Ryle at least, a con-
flict does arise as follows: Words for Ryle, at least in the second
paper cited, have uses (usually more than one, of course); sentences
do not. He more or less must maintain this position as strongly as
this to maintain that there is a category difference. Yet on the
Illocutionary Theory, sentences do have uses (often, but certainly
not always, more than one); that is, sentences may be used to do
certain things (i.e., with certain illocutions) and not others.

The obvious objection to this statement is that USE as used here is
equivocal as between the use of words and of sentences (though
Ryle, in the paper cited, does say quite categorically that sentences
have no uses). This objection is, I think, neither correct nor incorrect, but a gross over-simplification. My task now will be to make a
start on sorting out exactly how things stand in this area.

#3   We must first notice that Ryle has made what appears to be a
mistake, though not a very important one, when he says that sentences have no uses. There are certain obvious idiomatic sentences
which appear to have quite definite uses: *How are you, How do you
do, He went for a Burton* and so on. In answer to this I think that
Ryle would say that he is exclusively interested in the tight sense of
use where anything which has a use must be capable of being misused and that though sentences perhaps have uses they cannot be
misused. This does fairly well against the Illocutionary Theorists
but not against the examples given above. Thus *How do you do* has
a use as a salutation on meeting but not as a salutation when parting, i.e., used as a salutation when parting it would be misused. A
person who waved goodbye and called *How do you do* would be
misusing *How do you do*. Ryle half recognizes this fact when he
speaks of "a block of words ... congealed into a phrase". But he
shows no appreciation of the fact that this applies to sentences as
well as phrases and that it is not a relatively odd occurrence, as the
welding together of words in the phrase *sea-lawyer* is, but a pheno-
menon which, when applied to sentences, explains an enormous
part of market-place talk. However, perhaps he would still want to
claim that the sort of misuse I have cited is not quite the right sort

and, though I do not see quite how he could substantiate this, it may be so. In any case, the error is relatively unimportant because it is quite possible to imagine a language (used by very unconventional people, doubtless) where no sentence had a use in this sense. Such a language would be different from our own in many ways but it would still be clearly recognizable as a language.

#4   However, there is more wrong with Ryle's thesis here than this possible error. He also offers us the dichotomy, which is the heart of the Category Difference Theory, between utterances on the one hand and words on the other. I wish to oppose this dichotomy by offering a trichotomy as follows: (i) words, (ii) open sentences and sentences, and (iii) utterances. I shall first substantiate this trichotomy by showing that open sentences, as open sentences, play a significant role in our language and that the statement of this role is not analysable into statements about only words and utterances. [4]

That open sentences are a necessary category of explanation for our language is not, I think, hard to show; we would have noticed it long ago had not various theories about the use of words made us constitutionally blind in this area.

I wish to argue for this thesis: that on a good many occasions, though not all, when philosophers have avowedly been talking about the use of words, they have in fact been talking about the use of open sentences. Let us consider a few of the theories about the use of words which have been much discussed lately (without bothering as to the truth of these theories): *Good*, it has been said, is used to commend. But this is blatantly untrue; there is no notion of commending in asking *Is this a good blanket?* nor in *Buy me a good blanket.* [5] The only claim which, e.g., Hare, attempts to establish is that a set of open sentences, among which the most obvious are *A is good* and *A is a good Y*, are used to commend. Similarly, it has been claimed that *know* is not used to state facts but to give

---

[4]   The argument following amounts to a further justification of the point made in Chapter 5 that engagement rules are completely necessary for a full semantic analysis.

[5]   See R. Searle, "Meaning and Speech Acts", *Philosophical Review* (1962).

someone one's word, offer a guarantee, risk one's arm. But this is blatantly untrue; there is no notion of guaranteeing in *Do you know the gun is loaded?* or in *I know but I won't tell you* and precious little in *I know London*. The only claim which, e.g., Austin, attempts to establish is that the open sentence *I know (that) S* (*S* a statement variable) is used to give someone one's word, offer a personal guarantee. All this is, of course, to say no more than that philosophers are concerned with the use of words in certain types of context and I wish to claim no more for it. But what is important to notice is that we could not state the positions given above without talking about words in certain types of contexts or of open sentences; and it must therefore be a category in our discussion of language. I shall, in what follows, talk about open sentences rather than words in certain types of contexts but only for convenience. In particular, it allows me to tackle the problem of whether open sentences have uses.

#5   For Ryle, USE is tied to MISUSE; he wishes to say that words have uses in the sense that they can also be misused. In this sense of USE it is hard to make a really convincing case that open sentences have a use or uses. There is a temptation to argue that they do. Consider the following example: someone says *I promise to do X* when he does not intend to do X; or says *I know that S* when he does not even believe that S is true and has no reasons to do so; or says *I order you to Y* when he has no authority to do so. Something is the matter with utterances of these types; they are, as Austin would say, unhappy. But USE is such a broad term that no policeman's whistle would blow if we said they are misuses, though Ryle's whistle would. Ryle should carry the day here, I think, just because the sort of MISUSE noticed above is clearly different from the sort when words are misused; the ones above are more like ABUSEs than MISUSEs (what in fact goes wrong in this type of case is discussed below). Let us say, granting that saying it is both not without reasons and also somewhat legislative, that open sentences have uses, without any doubt, but they do not have uses in the sense where they can also be misused.

To say this appears to distinguish neatly between the sorts of uses words have and sorts of uses open sentences (and most sentences) have. It was clearly this that Ryle had in mind when he wrote "Ordinary Language". But the possibility of the distinction in these terms rests on the position that all words have a use or uses in the sense where misuse is possible; and this position, I shall claim, is false.

#6   All the words in the language have uses in some sense of USE; this is merely trivially true relying, as it does, on the enormous breadth of the notion of USE. However, USE in this highly general sense is just no good as a philosophical tool or in our search for the notion of meaning, even where there is a possible notion of misuse. For instance, words have what might be called grammatical uses, i.e., the grammar of our language is such that words can only fit into sentences in certain ways in virtue of their grammatical type. When a grammatical mistake has been made (what some might want to call a 'grammatical misuse'), no interesting semantic point hangs by it; the mistake just needs correcting before semantically interesting investigations can begin.   When we have a 'sentence' which is not grammatically well formed, like *Cat the of at brown*, it is not that one or more words have been misused in interesting ways, we just do not have a piece of English. That is, semantic or philosophical questions about the use of words just do not arise when a putative sentence is not grammatically well formed.

Similarly, all sorts of things can go wrong with utterances without there being a misuse of words. In particular, utterances can fail or be unhappy in certain ways because the conditions of their happiness are absent, i.e., the statement or statements which the happiness of a given statement presupposes may not be true. Thus I cannot marry a goat however many times I say *I do*; *Bring the horse from the barn* is unhappy, without there being any misuse of words, when there is no horse in the barn; *Hand me that book* fails to come off if I utter it while pointing at a flower (or pointing two ways at once); and so on. These sorts of unhappiness in utterances are interesting and important in their own right but they do not constitute misuse of words; in general terms, they constitute the failure of our utterances to mesh with a given situation such that we were foolish or ignorant or perverse in that we uttered them. What has gone wrong in these cases can be stated generally as follows: with very many types of utterances, the utterance fails to come off, is unhappy, if certain statements (certain presupposed statements) are not true. Thus the marriage formula only works when it is a person one is trying to marry and the request *Hand me the flowers on the table* is only happy when there are flowers on the table, and so on. To say that utterances are only happy under these conditions is not to say that they are only meaningful under these conditions; utterances may well be meaningful and, when uttered, achieve some aim (usually deceptive in some way) even if they are unhappy.

#7   However, what we must notice here is this: that even with the sorts of exceptions noted above, it is still only true that, though all words in the language have a use or uses in some sense of USE, this is trivially true because it relies on the enormous breadth of the notion of USE. We must make some finer distinctions here.

Some words, what earlier I called Category I words, have a use in the sense that they have an application. That is, the word *table* has an application, i.e., is applicable to certain articles of furniture, though every time it appears in a meaningful sentence of the language it need not be applied to one of these articles of furniture. Thus in the utterance *Is that a table?*, *table* is not applied to anything at all, and if someone says *That's a table*, pointing to a chair, he has misapplied *table*. However, for those words which have a use in that they have an application, there is no logical distinction between misapplying the word and speaking falsely. To put it another way, to say a word in a given sentence has been misapplied is just another way of saying the sentence is false, though it may locate what is false about it more clearly than merely saying it is false does. For example, to say that the utterance *The cat is on the mat* is false says less than saying *That's no cat; that's a lion* (in the formal mode, *You have misapplied 'cat'; that's a lion*), but that is hardly strange.

There is a further type of infelicity which encompasses what might be called misuses. Surprisingly enough, Ryle appears to have this type in mind some of the time in "Ordinary Language" when he speaks of misuse. Sometimes, when a word is used, it can fairly be said not to be the *mot juste*. That is, to call a piece of pop art *a picture* seems not quite right: it is not the sort of thing which comes to mind when we speak of pictures. Similarly, if a cross between a cat and a dog were somehow produced, it would doubtless be not quite right to call it a cat or a dog; we would not really know what to call it. Perhaps if it happened often enough we would have to invent a new word or change the meaning of an old one. This, I take it, is Ryle's notion of NON-STOCK or NON-STANDARD. We might call it THE CATEGORY OF THE NOT QUITE RIGHT.[6] This category is, in general, a very broad and interesting one which includes in its membership both words with applications and open sentences with functions. To see that it also includes open sentences, consider the now famous woman who knows her son is dead but does not believe it. He was killed in the war. She received official notification from the Government and very kind letters from his commanding officer and one of his friends, both of whom witnessed the tragedy. It is not that he is 'missing', he was killed. All this she knows. Yet each day she looks at her mail with expectation and each phone call she receives she expects to be from him. She cannot believe that he is really dead. Yet there is something not quite right here about employing the open sentence *She knows that S* and something equally not quite right in employing the open sentence *She believes that not-S*. Perhaps if this situation occurred more often we would preempt some special idiom (open sentence) to cover such cases but as it is we really do not know what to say. There is nothing odd about this. That is, there is no a priori reason to suppose our language is such that we have words or idioms suitable to every conceivable happening as the mot juste, and every empirical reason to

[6] The category of the not quite right comes about in this way. It will be recalled that words are, at least sometimes, surrounded by engagement rules (Chapter 5). When a word is used such that it seriously breaks one or more, but not all, of the engagement rules surrounding it, then that use will fall into the category of the not quite right.

suppose we have not. But we must note that it is odd to think of the category of the not quite right as constituting misuses of words or open sentences; they are just untypical uses. To call untypical uses misuses itself seems to be not quite right . What we have here, after all, is a failure of richness in our language such that every sort of situation which can conceivably occur cannot be adequately and shortly described in a word or a phrase. And that this should be the case is not surprising.

#8   It is now worthwhile to review the various types of infelicities so far discussed.

1. All words have grammatical uses in the sense that they fit correctly, in a grammatical sense, into sentences in certain ways and not in others. But when a putative sentence is not grammatically well formed no misuse of words has occurred, only a grammatical mistake or error. Notably when a sentence is not grammatically well formed it is a matter of judgement or guessing most of the time as to which word has been used wrongly. So it is, essentially, putative sentences which must be criticised for not being grammatically well formed, not words which can be said to suffer grammatical misuses.

2. A good many open sentences have uses in that they can be used to achieve certain aims. *X is a good Y*, most of the time at least, succeeds in commending Xs in the class of Ys; *I know that S*, most of the time at least, succeeds in laying the speaker's reputation on the line to the effect *that S*. But there is no possibility of misuse here in any tight sense. When we can be criticised in using these, and many other, open sentences it is because our use of one of them fails to mesh with a given situation such that we were foolish or ignorant or perverse in that we uttered it. With very many open sentences, the use of an instantiation of one of them fails to come off, is unhappy, when certain presupposed statements are not true.

3. A good many words have application, though they do not have to be applied to be meaningful, and can, of course, be misapplied. These words have clear possible misuses, namely when they are misapplied. But this form of misuse has the interesting

property that in the general instance there is no distinction between misapplying a word and speaking falsely. (In normal situations we can, of course, frequently distinguish between a misapplication and a false statement. But we do this by assessing, or guessing at, the speaker's intentions; it is nothing in the nature of language which allows us to make the distinction.)

4. There are untypical uses of words and open sentences: uses which fall into the category of the not quite right.

These classes of uses of words and open sentences, with their attendant infelicities where applicable, are not the sort of thing philosophers appear to have in mind when they speak about use and misuse. That is, there seem to be strong indications in the frequently inexplicit writings on the subject that it is misuses which are not grammatical misuses of words, nor the inappropriateness of an open sentence to do the job in hand, nor a misapplication, nor yet merely untypical uses which they have in mind when they speak of misuses. But what do they have in mind?

At least one sort of thing they have in mind is this: such misuses as the use of *true* in the posited utterance *That is a true argument*. We must first note that it is indeterminate in this utterance which word is being misused; substitution of a different word for *true*, namely *valid*, would remove the misuse, but so would substitution of *statement* for *argument*. However, the heart of the difficulty does not lie there. The word *true* is a word with an application; so is the word *argument*. But the phrase *true argument* can be correctly applied to nothing; it is not just that either *true* or *argument* is misapplied, it is that the phrase *true argument*, the way our language is now constituted, can never be correctly applied to anything as a matter of logic nor of fact.[7] Thus one can get cases of misapplication of a word or words which are different from most misapplication in this sense: that it is only the case, as a matter of fact, that a misapplication has taken place but it is necessarily the case that in

---

[7] This type of misuse comes about as follows. It will be recalled that words are surrounded by entailment rules (Chapter 5). When it is the case that the words in a phrase of this type have associated with them entailment rules and any two apodoses of their entailment rules contradict one another, then this sort of logical impossibility of correct application will arise.

the posited utterance offered the phrase cannot fail to be misapplied. With most misapplications, the sentence uttered could be uttered in circumstances such that there is no misapplication, but in this case the sentence can never be uttered such that there is no misapplication.

This sort of case is interesting in its own right but it is clear that it does not reveal a new possibility of misuse but a special possibility of misapplication. A notion of misuse of words different from grammatical misuses, misapplications and untypical uses still eludes us.

There is, I think, good reason why it eludes us: it does not exist. That is, if we have before us an utterance which is a grammatically well formed sentence then the only things which can be wrong with it in philosophically interesting ways are that various words in it might be misapplied or used untypically, or an open sentence of which it is an instantiation might be improperly employed. In no other sense can there be a misuse. But it should be noticed that my thesis here is not as iconoclastic as it sounds. Although it can be phrased as above there is a less contentious way of phrasing it, namely to say that what philosophers have in the past called misuses are not one category but many. In particular, to speak of misuse when a sentence is not grammatically well formed is clearly reasonable; equally, misapplications occur and, more particularly, necessary misapplications (*true argument*), and these are certainly misuses; and inappropriate types of sentences (i.e., inappropriate open sentences) are on occasions employed and these can, with some plausibility, be called misuses; and the flux of experience is sufficiently capable of variation that the occurrence of untypical uses of words and open sentences is doubtless inevitable, though this hardly qualifies as a genuine misuse. My claim here is that these types of misuse are very different and that there are no more philosophically interesting types. None of this fits in with the Category Difference Theory.

I shall now sum up the difficulties which there appear to be in the Category Difference Theory: Ryle holds that there is a dichotomy in language between words which have uses, in the sense where misuse is possible, and sentences which have no uses in this sense. I have argued that there is a trichotomy as follows: (i) words, some of which but not all of which have uses in the sense where misuse is possible; (ii) open sentences which have uses, but not in the required sense; and sentences, a few of which seem to have uses in the required sense; and (iii) utterances, which do not have uses in the required sense. If I am correct in these contentions then the notion of use where misuse is possible, though very important, is useless as a means of categorizing bits of language in the way Ryle wants; in addition, the Category Difference Theory is wrong because the mechanisms for its defining distinction break down. More particularly, the Category Difference Theory is wrong, or incoherent, where it conflicts with the Illocutionary Theory.

However, that does not imply that the Illocutionary Theory is correct.

#9   The Illocutionary Theory suffers from difficulties which are, in many ways, the converse of the difficulties in the Category Difference Theory. Where Ryle appears to centre all interest on individual words, utterances being generated from words and meaning what they do mean in virtue of the uses of these words, the Illocutionary Theorists (especially Alston) centre all attention on the function of utterances. Certainly it is a persuasive idea when one is in full flight from the notion that the prime function of language is to state facts. Consider the sorts of lists of illocutions usually given as examples: apologizing, marrying, promising, questioning, commanding, and so on. With the first two of these, it is easy to persuade oneself that any utterance which has one of these illocutions is virtually synonymous with any other that has the same illocution; the meanings of such utterances seem to derive very largely from their functions or illocutions. With the last three, the same considerations seem to apply to the open sentences involved (e.g., *I promise to do X*). But even at this stage there is a difficulty apparently not noticed by philosophers who espouse this idea, a difficulty very like the old difficulty of the difference between sense and reference. That is, just as *the Morning Star* and *the Evening Star* refer to the same object but mean different things, so *I wish I hadn't done it* and *I am sorry I did it*, said in circumstances which make it plain that they are both apologies, achieve the same object but appear to mean different things.

However, it is not necessary to push this point because there are other areas where the Illocutionary Theory glaringly will not do. The theory fits give-and-take conversation a great deal better than it does extended utterances or writing (which is hardly accidental, presumably, with the attention which linguists have lately been giving to speech rather than literature). That is, in most conversations, each utterance by each speaker tends to have relatively well defined illocution and much of the communicative nature of what is said is understood once this illocution is grasped. It is in this area that the theory has real plausibility.

#10   However, we must also consider extended discourse. To take a fairly concrete example, let us consider an extended description of some fairly large and complex object (e.g., an old castle). Let us suppose that the body of this description consists (as is the case with paradigm descriptions) in quite a large set of statements of fact about the object being described. The illocution of each of these statements will be FACT STATING, STATING or, perhaps, DESCRIBING. (DESCRIBING is dubious because any one fact does not, as a rule, describe an object, though it may well contribute to the description of the object). As the illocution, if given as FACT STATING, is the same for all the statements and all, presumably, mean something different, meaning cannot lie in the illocution so designated (though the meaning of the utterance is, of course, logically connected in its illocution). Perhaps, therefore, the illocution should be given in more detail. Thus the illocution of *The walls are grey* might be given as *stating the colour of the walls*. But this still fails to catch the meaning of the statement just because it would also cover *The walls are pink*. The illocution of *The walls are grey*, if the meaning of the utterance is to be caught by the illocution, must be *stating that the walls are grey*. Apart from the fact that this sort of extended clause is not the sort of thing propounders of the Illocutionary Theory ever show signs of having in mind for the category of illocutions, it still will not do. Or else it will do but is trivial. That is, to give the meaning of an utterance by repeating it in a form of indirect speech only gives the meaning of the utterance in a trivial sense, though how the original utterance is put into indirect speech does give its illocution (which is, of course, logically connected with the meaning of the utterance). Thus, to say that the meaning of the utterance *The walls are grey* is given by saying that the illocution is *stating that the walls are grey* is to say (a) that the sentence *The walls are grey* was used, on this occasion, in a fact stating (or, perhaps, describing,) capacity, i.e., that its illocution on this occasion of its use is STATING, and (b) that it means what it does mean. It also stretches the notion of illocution to vacuity. The way ILLOCUTION is usually (and usefully) used, the utterance *The walls are grey* has both a meaning and an illocution, not just an illocution which carries the meaning somehow within it. To return to the example, in a description of the type postulated every statement means something (probably different) but all the statements have the same illocution. The only information we get from knowing the illocution of an utterance is how the given sentence, on this occasion of its utterance, is being used; it does not necessarily tell us much about the meaning of the utterance except in those highly colloquial areas of language use where sentences (or open sentences) tend to have only one possible illocution (*I promise to do X* being of this type).

#11 The Category Difference Theory and the Illocutionary Theory are, then, both incorrect, though both point up interesting aspects of the way utterances are meaningful. In addition, in so far as the Wittgensteinian theory mentioned at the beginning of this Appendix is a theory at all, it is incorrect if what has been said about the notion of USE above is correct.

With some diffidence, I would like to suggest that these three theories are obviously wrong. The supposition that all words or all sentences or all utterances are meaningful in the same way is just ridiculous. The word *damn* is clearly meaningful in a way different from the way in which the word *autobiography* or the word *as* is meaningful and any theory which makes them all meaningful in the same way is going to be either false or empty. The same considerations apply to sentences and utterances. The ways in which our utterances are meaningful are very various and it is going to be a long, detailed and hard-working task to sort them out. I have made a very small beginning in deliberately circumscribed cases in different places in this monograph. But it must be emphasized that this is only the smallest of small beginnings.

BIBLIOGRAPHY

Alston, William P., "Meaning and Use", *Philosophical Quarterly*, 13 (1963).
——, *Philosophy of Language* (Englewood Cliffs, 1964).
Austin, J. L., *Philosophical Papers* (Oxford, 1961).
——, *Sense and Sensibilia* (Oxford, 1962).
——, *How To Do Things with Words* (Oxford, 1962).
Chomsky, Noam, *Syntactic Structures* (The Hague, 1957).
——, "A Transformational Approach to Syntax", *Proceedings of the Third Texas Conference on Problems of Linguistic Analysis of English* (Austin, Texas, 1962).
——, Reprinted in *The Structure of Language*, ed. J. Fodor and J. Katz (Englewood Cliffs, 1964).
——, *Aspects of the Theory of Syntax* (Cambridge, Mass., 1965).
Fries, C. C., *The Structure of English* (London, 1952).
Katz, J., *The Philosophy of Language* (New York, 1966).
Hare, R. M., *The Language of Morals* (Oxford, 1952).
Ryle, Gilbert, *The Concept of Mind* (London, 1949).
——, "Ordinary Language", *Philosophical Review*, LXII (1953). Reprinted in *Ordinary Language*, ed. V. C. Chappell (Englewood Cliffs, 1964).
——, "The Theory of Meaning", *British Philosophy at the Mid-Century*, ed. C. A. Mace (London, 1957).
——, "Use, Usage and Meaning", *Proceedings of the Aristotelian Society*, supplementary volume xxxv (1961).
Searle, R., "Meaning and Speech Acts", *Philosophical Review*, LXXI (1962).
Wheatley, Jon, "Like", *Proceedings of the Aristotelian Society*, N.S. LXII (1962-62).
——, "How to Give a Word a Meaning", *Theoria*, XXX (1964).
——, "Logical Connection", *American Philosophical Quarterly*, 4 (1967).
——, "Entrenchment and Engagement", *Analysis*, 27 (1967).
Wittgenstein, L., *Philosophical Investigations* (Oxford, 1953).

INDEX

JANUA LINGUARUM

STUDIA MEMORIAE NICOLAI VAN WIJK DEDICATA
Edited by C. H. van Schooneveld

SERIES MINOR

35. LUIS J. PRIETO: Principes de noologie: Fondements de la théorie fonctionnelle du signifié. Préface d'André Martinet. 1964. 130 pp., 36 figs. Gld. 21.—
36. SEYMOUR CHATMAN: A Theory of Meter. 1965. 229 pp., many graphs, 2 plates. Gld. 23.—
37. WAYNE TOSH: Syntactic Translation. 1965. 162 pp., 58 figs. Gld. 23.—
38. NOAM CHOMSKY: Current Issues in Linguistic Theory. 1964. 119 pp. Gld. 12.—
39. D. CRYSTAL and R. QUIRK: Systems of Prosodic and Paralinguistic Features in English. 1964. 94 pp., 16 plates. Gld. 14.—
40. FERENC PAPP: Mathematical Linguistics in the Soviet Union. 1966. 165 pp. Gld. 24.—
41. S. K. ŠAUMJAN: Problems of Theoretical Phonology. 1968. 224 pp. some figs. Gld. 26.—
42. MILKA IVIĆ: Trends in Linguistics. Translated by Muriel Heppell. 1965. 260 pp. Gld. 28.—
43. ISTVÁN FODOR: The Rate of Linguistic Change: Limits of the Application of Mathematical Methods in Linguistics. 1965. 85 pp., some figs. Gld. 13.—
44. THEODORE M. DRANGE: Type Crossings: Sentential Meaninglessness in the Border Area of Linguistics and Philosophy. 1966. 218 pp. Gld. 23.—
45. WARREN H. FAY: Temporal Sequence in the Perception of Speech. 1966. 126 pp., 29 figs. Gld. 19.50
46. A. CAPELL: Studies in Socio-Linguistics. 1966. 167 pp., 2 tables. Gld. 22.—
47. BOWMAN CLARKE: Language and Natural Theology. 1966. 181 pp. Gld. 26.—
49. SAMUEL ABRAHAM and FERENC KIEFER: A Theory of Structural Semantics. 1966. 98 pp., 20 figs. Gld. 15.—
50. ROBERT J. SCHOLES: Phonotactic Grammatically. 1966. 117 pp., many figs. Gld. 15.—
51. HOWARD R. POLLIO: The Structural Basis of Word Association Behavior. 1966. 96 pp., 4 folding tables. 8 pp. graphs, figs. Gld. 16.—
52. JEFFREY ELLIS: Towards and General Comparative Linguistics. 1966. 170 pp. Gld. 22.—
54. RANDOLPH QUIRK and JAN SVARTVIK: Investigating Linguistic Acceptability. 1966. 118 pp., 14 figs., 4 tables. Gld. 15.—
55. THOMAS A. SEBEOK (ED.): Selected Writings of Gyula Laziczius. 1966. 226 pp. Gld. 26.—
56. NOAM CHOMSKY: Topics in the Theory of Generative Grammar. 1966. 96 pp. Gld. 12.—
58. LOUIS G. HELLER and JAMES MACRIS: Parametric Linguistics. 1967. 80 pp., 23 tables. Gld. 10.—

59. JOSEPH H. GREENBERG: Language Universals: With Special Reference to Feature Hierarchies. 1966. 89 pp.   Gld. 18.—

60. CHARLES F. HOCKETT: Language, Mathematics, and Linguistics. 1967. 244 pp., some figs.   Gld. 21.—

62. B. USPENSKY: Principles of Structural Typology. 1968. 80 pp.   Gld. 14.—

63. V. Z. PANFILOV: Grammar and Logic. 1968. 160 pp.   Gld. 16.—

64. JAMES C. MORRISON: Meaning and Truth in Wittgenstein's Tractatus. 1968. 148 pp.   Gld. 18.—

65. ROGER L. BROWN: Wilhelm von Humboldt's Conception of Linguistic Relativity. 1967. 132 pp.   Gld. 16.—

66. EUGENE J. BRIERE: A Psycholinguistic Study of Phonological Interference. 1968. 84 pp.   Gld. 12.—

67. ROBERT L. MILLER: The Linguistic Relativity Principle and New Humboldtian Ethnolinguistics: A History and Appraisal 1968. 127 pp.   Gld. 16.—

69. I. M. SCHLESINGER: Sentence Structure and the Reading Process. 1968. 172 pp.   Gld. 18.—

70. A. ORTIZ and E. ZIERER: Set Theory and Linguistics. 1968. 64 pp.   Gld. 10.—

71. HANS-HEINRICH LIEB: Communication Complexes and Their Stages. 1968. 140 pp.   Gld. 17.—

72. ROMAN JAKOBSON: Child Language, Aphasia and Phonological Universals. 1968. 104 pp.   Gld. 12.—

73. CHARLES F. HOCKETT: The State of the Art. 1968. 124 pp. Gld. 14.—

74. A. JUILLAND and HANS-HEINRICH LIEB: "Klasse" und Klassifikation in der Sprachwissenschaft. 1968. 75 pp.   Gld. 13.—

76. URSULA OOMEN: Automatische Syntaktische Analyse. 1968. 84 pp.   Gld. 16.—

MOUTON · PUBLISHERS · THE HAGUE